Lotus Illustrated DICTIONARY of ART

Compiled and Edited by:

Paul Harding

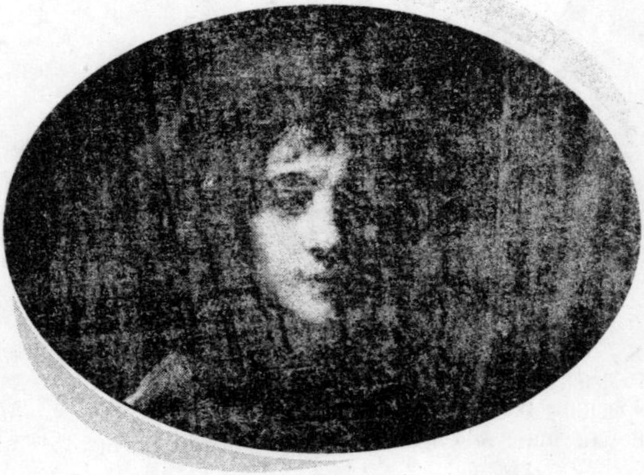

Lotus PRESS
4735/22,Prakash Deep Building
Ansari Road, Darya Ganj,
New Delhi-110002

Lotus *Illustrated*

DICTIONARY *of* ART

ISBN 81 89093 13 4

Published by:
Lotus Press : Publishers & Distributors
Unit No. 220, 2nd Floor, 4735/22,
Prakash Deep Building, Ansari Road, Darya Ganj,
New Delhi- 110002, Ph.: 32903912, 23280047, 09811838000
• E-mail : lotus_press@sify.com www.lotuspress.co.in

Printed at : ***Concept Imprint,*** Delhi

PREFACE

Art is a disciplined activity that may be limited to skill or expanded to include a distinctive way of looking at the world. The word art is derived from the Latin ars, which means 'skill'. Art is therefore the skill of performing a set of specialised actions, like the art of gardening or of playing chess. In a broader sense, art comprises of both skill and creative imagination in a musical, literary, visual or performance context. Art provides its practitioners and learners with an aesthetic, emotional and intellectual experience.

Conventionally, in many societies, art acted towards combining both practical and aesthetic functions. But, around the 18th century in the West, people began to distinguish between art that was purely aesthetic and art that was also practical. The aesthetics primarily consisted of literature, music, dance, painting, sculpture and architecture, while the decorative or applied arts, such as pottery, metalwork, furniture, tapestry and enamel, although considered as useful arts, were for a time demoted to the rank of crafts.

This dictionary is an attempt to bring all the important terms that are used in the field of art under one head. The glossary discusses the art jargon in simplified terms, accompanied by appropriate pictures and examples, wherever required. The objective behind collating the myriad of art terms at one location was to provide the readers with a handy guide. This repertoire will equip the reader with the basic knowledge about art and thus help him/her enter the field without any inhibitions and hang-ups.

■ absence

an instance in which uncertainty about meaning prevails over the metaphysics of presence. The term lurks behind the received opinion of David Salle's paintings of the 1980s.

■ absolute

1. as a noun in general, anything free of dependence upon factors external to itself. In metaphysical idealism specifically, the totality of what in fact exists.

2. as an adjective in formal terminology, it has connotations related to the former. For example, 'absolute scale' means the actual size of an object, without reference to the size it appears to be in a given context.

■ absolutism

1. in aesthetics, the opposite of relativism, i.e., that there are, for example, eternal and immutable standards for the evaluation of works of art.

2. in politics, unrestricted political power. Postmodernism generally rejects all forms of absolutism.

■ abstraction

often used interchangeably with non- objective, more precisely, imagery which departs from representational accuracy for some affective or other purpose unrelated to verisimilitude. Abstraction has been treated to a good deal of revision by critics who practice a type of semiotics.

■ absurd

generally, a state of irrationality or meaninglessness. More specifically, absurdity is:

1. a flaw in logic.

2. a basic premise of existentialism which asserts that the meaning of the world does not precede the existence of beings capable of formulating a conception of meaning.

■ acceptability

the idea of acceptable standards, particularly of interpretation, is pretty much a taboo in generally postmodernist times, but if a criticism is tacitly an intelligent argument, then it is measurable by such standards. Of course, artwriters then have to agree on the criteria of acceptability, which they have not yet done. In conventional informal logic, acceptability is usually defined as sufficiency, validity and defensible premises for a given audience, which is ideally assumed to be a 'universal' audience of reasonable people.

■ accommodation

adaption or adjustment practiced by an individual, an ethnic group or the like, seeking admission or assimilation into a larger group, culture or social body of whatever sort.

■ acculturation

this can describe both cross-cultural (or intercultural) borrowing and the process by which persons acquire knowledge of the culture in which they live. Feminism and critiques of ethnocentrism make use of the term with slight variations.

■ accumulated intention

in The Principles of Semantics, Stephen Ullmann argues that words gather meanings unto themselves over time, producing not merely conventional ambiguity, but also the power of symbolic expression in general. Words and images thus function as accumulators of meaning. The idea could serve as a practical explanation of some of the more ephemeral results of deconstruction.

■ acrylic

a plastic-based painting medium, which, because it is water soluble, dries quickly and cleans up easily. Especially popular in the 1960s and 1970s for effects ranging from translucent watercolour-like washes to opaque hardedges in bright colours, acrylic seems to have been declining in popularity since the new image movement of the early 1980s restored interest in oil as a medium.

■ action painting

Harold Rosenberg's 1952 term for those works, within

the orbit of American abstract expressionism, which featured very energetically applied painting, apparently involving movements of the whole body or at least of its larger limbs, as opposed to minute movements of the fingers and wrist and a certain indifference to traditional niceties of execution, like the avoidance of drips and spatters. Rosenberg had the works of Willem de Kooning in mind because of the famous 1951 coverage in Life magazine of Jackson Pollock, in which Hans Namuth's photographs clearly show the artist dripping paint through the air onto a canvas on the floor. There are many other variations of action painting, including French tachisme and Canadian automatisme. Although in varying degrees, they have in common Rosenberg's notion that the canvas is 'an arena in which to act', rather than a distanced product of reflection and deliberation.

■ adbusters

see **culture jamming**.

■ add women and stir

an expression used by some feminists (see feminism) who feel that simply adding women to existing canons of artistic greatness really does nothing to challenge or change the processes of canon-formation, which are inherently hierarchical and sexist.

■ ad hominem

traditionally considered a fallacy, ad hominem is a usually pernicious type of argument which attempts to discredit a counter-argument by questioning the opponent, rather than the opponent's position: such-and-such person's views should not be given credence because his/her character is disreputable, s/he is not knowledgeable, trustworthy or unbiased, his/her credentials are not apparent or are irrelevant or there is no consensual agreement or resolution on the part of other authorities.

■ ad ignorantium

considered a flaw in reasoning, an ad ignorantium argument appeals to ignorance, as it were. One commits this error if, after failing to find evidence that a claim is true, one appeals to ignorance by concluding the claim is false or vice versa.

■ admissible

capable of being admitted, allowed, conceded, permitted and the like. In legal contexts, a great deal of attention is paid to what can and cannot be admitted as evidence, but only rarely is such attention given to the question in artwriting. This results in arguments and interpretations, which appear to be valid but are constructed on flimsy or irrelevant grounds.

■ adversarial

occasionally used in place of the adjective 'adversary', meaning 'having or involving antagonistic parties or interests'. It is a key component of the avant- garde and of bohemianism and some feel it has even become mainstream culture.

■ aegis

term used in Norman Bryson's Tradition and Desire to replace source analysis in traditional art history with a conception of allusion as a trope. Hypothetically, an artist uses an earlier artist's manner as a source to take refuge in and to challenge its authority.

■ aesthetic distance

1. the audience's awareness that art and reality are not the same, entailing some suspension of disbelief.

2. the term is sometimes used to refer to the distance between a completed art object and the circumstances of its production.

■ aesthetic emotion

see **unique aesthetic emotion**.

■ aestheticism

term often used to connote a certain decadence or preciousness.

aesthetics

originally, that which pertains to the beautiful, as conceived variously by artists and, especially, philosophers with reference to noble aspects of experience beyond superficial appearance or mere prettiness. The theme preoccupied philosophers in ancient Greece, but the term itself first appeared in the eighteenth-century writings of Alexander Baumgarten. Since the adoption of the term 'esthetician' to describe purveyors of cosmetics, 'aesthetics' seems to have little relevance, unless one thinks of it more generically as 'pertaining to the philosophy of art', i.e., its function, nature, ontology, purpose and so on. The term is still sometimes used to indicate a certain imprecise distinction between art and life or as a rough synonym for 'artistic'.

affective

pertaining to emotional expression.

ageism

on the model of racism and sexism, a discriminatory attitude against people because of their age.

agenda

a list or outline of things to do, issues to resolve, questions to be decided and the like. In popular post-modern parlance, especially when preceded by 'hidden', the word connotes premeditated cultural mechanisms of persuasion and/or repression.

aha experience

the literature of psychology describes the instant of insight and release, in puzzle or problem solving, as the aha experience. It would be useful to consider whether the type of satisfaction afforded by a particularly compelling interpretation corresponds to this in any meaningful way, since it would seem to imply that an artwork is principally something to 'figure out', rather than something to experience in an open-ended manner.

ahistorical

generally, that which is not concerned with history or historical development. It is sometimes used as a synonym for anachronism, particularly when the actions, ideas and/or motives of a given generation are attributed to an earlier one.

air brush

a device which sprays paint with compressed air, to offer a broad range of applications, from wide patches of paint to thin mists enabling precise details. The principle is the same whether one uses an inexpensive contraption with one's breath or a rather expensive mechanical version of a device invented in the late nineteenth century by Charles Burdick. Air brush painting was particularly popular in 1960s and 1970s advertising and van painting and its effect of photographic verisimilitude was adopted for use in pop art and photorealism.

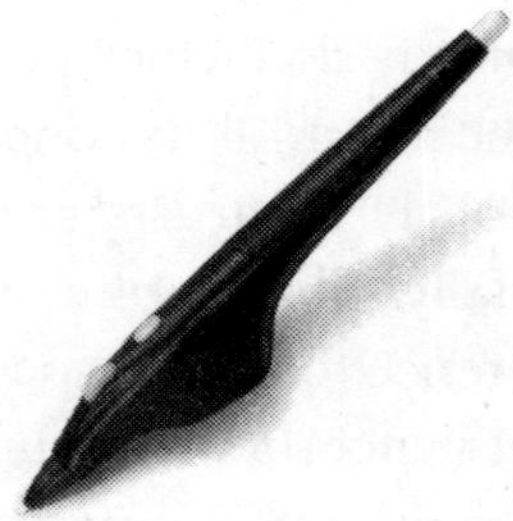

aleatoric

composition based on chance, usually, but sometimes also random accident and/or highly improvisational execution.

aletheia

originally a Greek term meaning 'truth' or 'the unconcealedness of things'. Current writers often use the word with the connotations supplied by Heidegger in The Origin of the Work of Art, in which an artwork is useful to the extent that it can open up a space in which existentially alienated beings can discover the meaning of their existence, which is not synonymous with 'truth' in the conventional sense.

■ alienation

sometimes generally used to suggest depersonalisation, disenchantment, estrangement or powerlessness, alienation is actually a philosophical word with a lengthy history. The most particular conceptions appear in Hegelianism, Marxism and existentialism. Simply put, in Hegel, alienations were various stages in the development of human consciousness: the lowest was immediate perception of sense data, the next a consciousness of self, the next the abstraction of reason and finally the world of the spirit, manifest in religion and art.

■ allegory

traditionally, a type of figurative expression, usually a narrative with one or more personifications and often with some moralising conclusion. More recently, it has been used in postmodernism to describe the relation of one text to another, particularly where they purport to be about the same thing but actually introduce unbidden levels of signification alien to each other.

■ allusion

passing reference to an event, object or person presumed to be familiar to the audience, most commonly to increase affective potential without extensive digression. As such, it is a less precise artistic borrowing than appropriation or citation. The wailing mother with the dead child in Picasso's Guernica, for example, may be understood as an ironic allusion to the typical Madonna and child.

■ altar

a structure on which sacrifices or other offerings were made to the gods. In Christian tradition, although the altar serves more to allude to the table at which the Last Supper took place, the celebration of the mystery of the Eucharist, i.e., that bread and wine are the body and blood of Christ, is still a sacrificial affair of sorts. Altars are a central part of many forms of religious life and are accordingly given special visual treatment with such things as altarpieces.

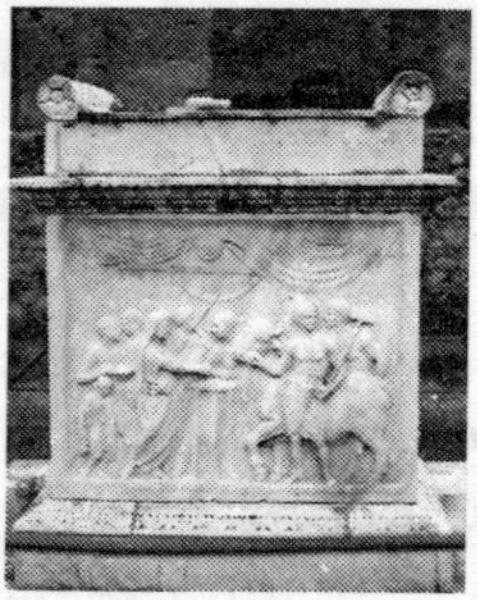

■ **altarpiece**

any of a variety of decorated panels, screens or shrines rising behind an altar to signify its importance and authority, to tell an associated legend and so on. The most common type of altarpiece is a painting spread over several panels, hung together like folding screens. A simple type consists of a central panel with two flanking half-sized doors to close over it. A three-part painting of this sort is called a triptych. Paintings with more complicated arrangements, as in Van Eyck's celebrated Ghent Altarpiece, are called polyptychs. Altarpieces often have a decorated panel at the bottom called a predella.

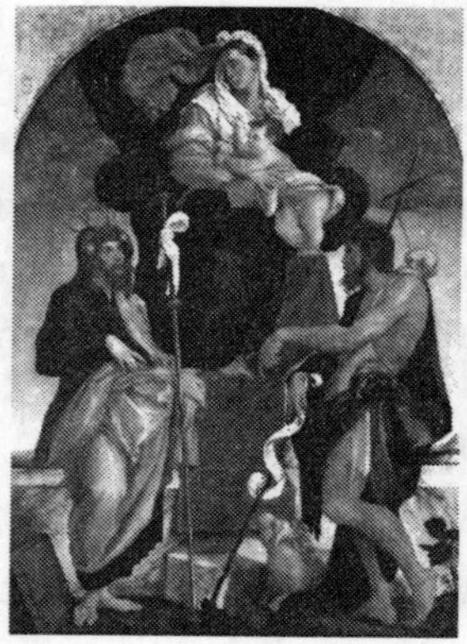

■ **alterity**

not to be confused with altarity, alterity is the condition of being radically different or unlike some other being, state or thing.

■ **alternating figures**

ambiguous diagrams serving in the psychology of perception to illustrate the way the mind habitually tries to achieve a coherent Gestalt. An example is the famous impossible trident, the bottom half of which seems like a square 'u' and the top half like three prongs.

■ altersstil
German term referring to the style of an artist in old age, especially when it has characteristics distinguishing it from earlier parts of the artist's career. Notable examples include late Michelangelo and Titian.

■ althusserian
pertaining to the ideas of philosopher Louis Althusser.

■ always-already-read
Frederic Jameson argues that no text exists in a vacuum, for when it is read by a member of an identifiable social group, its meaning is mediated by his or her ideology. The material is thus always already read, in a sense. For visual art, there is no need to transform the term to 'always-already-seen', because the component 'seen' implies a value-free physiological phenomenon, which postmodernism generally dismisses.

■ ambiguity
something which admits of interpretation in two or more possible senses. In logical and critical texts, ambiguity is usually something to be avoided, but many creative works capitalise on it quite effectively. There are, for instance, ambiguities of drawing in Matisse's Le Luxe II and ambiguities of content in Dorothea Tanning's Birthday.

■ ambivalence
often colloquially known as 'mixed feelings', mildly conflicting emotions or contradictory attitudes.

■ ambulatory
an aisle surrounding the altar at the apse end of a church or a covered passage around an open court, as in a cloister.

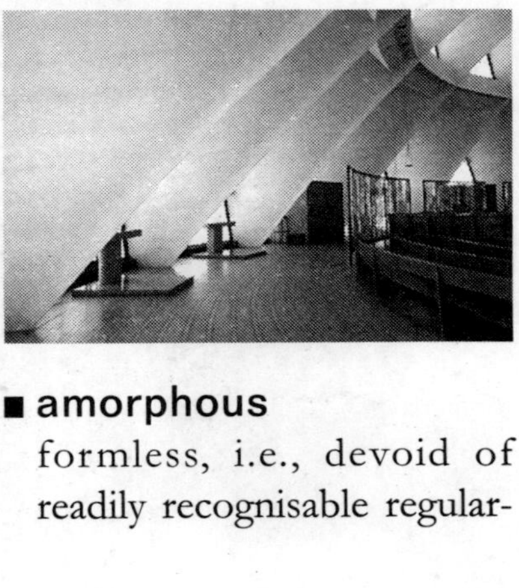

■ amorphous
formless, i.e., devoid of readily recognisable regular-

ity in form, as in a standard shape like a rectangle or a triangle.

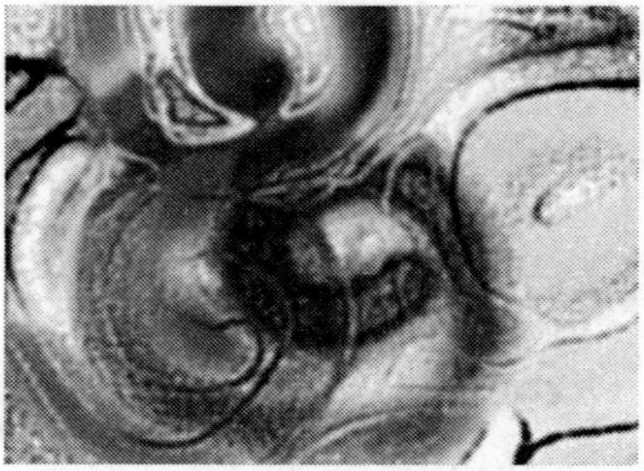

■ **amphora**

a large storage jar with a fairly tall neck and two handles stretching from a wide mouth to a broader oval body. In Greek antiquity, such jars were for both practical and trophy purposes. Without their painted depictions of the Greek myths, we would have very little knowledge of ancient Greek pictorial practice.

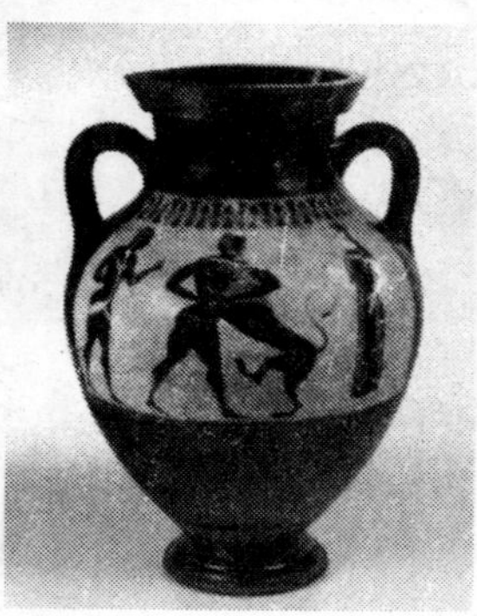

■ **anachronism**

chronological misplacement, usually running backwards in time, as in asserting that Freud used a CD player or some such thing.

■ **analepsis**

the recovery into consciousness of unconscious, repressed or forgotten material. Clear examples are in Max Ernst's descriptions of the discovery of frottage and Salvador Dali's paranoiac-critical method.

■ **analogy**

a comparison in which two things have sufficient numbers of similar characteristics to conclude that they will probably share others. It is commonly used when a familiar thing is used to explain something less familiar and as such is a basic component of symbolism.

■ **analytic psychology**

Jungian term for a wholistic type of depth psychology which takes into account not only the collective unconscious and the personal unconscious as motivators of behaviour, but also the conscious aspirations and goals of the subject. A hypothetical criticism so inspired would differ fundamentally from Freudian-based psychoanalytical criticism.

■ anamorphosis

mannered or distorted imagery that can be optically corrected by examining it from an unconventional point of view or through some optical device. Although the term usually indicates a simple visual example of the phenomenon, as in Hans Holbein's The Ambassadors, Donald Preziosi uses it in Rethinking Art History as a metaphor of the way historical narrative deforms the object of investigation.

■ anchorage and relay

Roland Barthes' characterisation of the functions of captions in advertising, the former serving to anchor (i.e., delimit) the meanings of the example, for example, via identification and the latter serving to proliferate meaning via a process of referral to other absent significances.

■ anchoring gaze

in You Just Don't Understand, Deborah Tannen coined this term to indicate the principal line of sight of people in conversation. She found that female speakers tended to face one another and look directly into each other's faces, whereas male speakers tended to sit at angles to each other and find visual home bases elsewhere in the room. The idea gives further support to her distinction between rapport-talk and report-talk. The idea might be exploited to disrupt the simple polarity of Bryson's gaze and glance.

■ androcentric

a specifically male anthropocentrism. A typical, though simple example is the use of the word 'man' to refer to both genders. Imagine how it might be used to discuss the canon of art history.

anima
originally, the soul or life force, but now universally construed as the Jungian archetype of the female components within a male personality. Presumably, a male projects his own female side, whether it be creatively inspiring (the muse) or protective and nurturing (the mother), etc., onto those around him. Jung designated the reverse, the male components within a female personality, as animus, but he did not explore the concept to as great a depth.

animus
see **anima**.

anosagnosia
a neurological term coined by Babinski, a contemporary of Freud, designating certain patients' inability to know they are suffering from a cognitive deficit, particularly agnosia. Such patients thus have a double deficit, for they have even lost an awareness of their loss.

antagonist
in narrative analysis, the adversary or opponent of the protagonist.

anthropocentrism
the mind-set that sees human beings as central (i.e., essential and most significant) in the universe.

anthropomorphism
the representation of non-human beings, whether real or fictitious, in human form (e.g., the gods). The ascription of human attributes, characteristics and/or pre-occupations to non-human beings (e.g., the speaking animals in Aesop's fables).

anti-aesthetic
the title of an influential postmodernist anthology edited by Hal Foster (1983), in which he expressly argues that 'anti-aesthetic' does not mean a reassertion of modernism's principle of aesthetic negation or anti-art, but rather a critique of the very notion of the aesthetic, especially in its modern manifestations with suppos-

edly pseudotranshistorical and determinate meanings.

anti-art

imprecise but once fashionable term to describe works which sought to denounce or dismantle traditional conceptions of art, whether through untraditional techniques, materials and display formats (e.g., automatism, combine painting, installation) or through unusual iconography and the like.

anti-authoritarian

the essential characteristic of any challenge to presumed authority.

anti-intellectualism

any position, whether originating with an unreflective street tough or a philosophical pragmatist, which eschews, fears or mistrusts reason. Some hyper- intellectual artwriting is, paradoxically, overtly anti- intellectual.

antinomianism

originally, the doctrine that moral laws do not apply to Christ. By extension, the notion that certain persons with privileged status do not have to obey their own dictates, as in 'Do as I say, not as I do'. Many artists, especially those of the middle class who feign distaste for bourgeois values, have exhibited such characteristics.

antinomy

a paradox or contradiction between two conclusions, both of which were apparently arrived at by proper reasoning.

antinomy of distance

Edward Bullough's conception of aesthetic distance includes a paradox of sorts: an artist's work will be most powerful when it is most personal, but s/he can only formulate an effective artistic expression by assuming a certain detachment from it. Similarly, a viewer's experience of a work of art will be augmented if s/he has experienced something similar, but if a certain aesthetic distance is not maintained, the art is superseded by the viewer's own emotional state.

antiphrasis
a specific type of irony in which a sign is used to signal its opposite.

antiquarianism
originally, the study of the material culture of ancient societies, particularly those whose current descendants exhibit markedly different customs, as in Egypt. In certain circles, the term now has a connotation of commercialism and commodity exchange for profit, rather than for the expansion of the frontiers of knowledge.

antithesis
1. a single figure with markedly contrasting ideas.
2. the second component of the Hegelian dialectic.

antonomasia
a figure in which a general idea is represented by a proper name, as when artists' names signify their entire oeuvre or an unspecified single work. This is everywhere in art criticism, art history, etc.

aorist
literally 'without horizons', the term designates a classical Greek tense presenting an occurrence without limitation as to duration.

aphasia
impairment of the ability to use and/or understand words.

aphorism
a concise statement of a principle or something held by the speaker to be true or deeply felt.

apophasis
the rhetorical figure in which one states something while seeming to deny it. The phrases 'not to mention such and such' and 'to make a long story short' are apophasis.

apophatic
a theological term meaning knowledge of God obtained by negation. Much modernism has been apophatic inasmuch as the autonomy of art has been asserted chiefly by

excluding what art is not. Since what 'art is not' is really what 'art is thought not to be', there is a similar dimension of faith involved.

■ aporia

formerly, a type of irony in which certainty, say, about a person's character, masquerades as deferential uncertainty. Now the term is more likely to mean the point at which a text is most explicitly indeterminate or self-contradictory, as in deconstruction.

■ apostrophe

a figure in which something or someone is addressed in their absence. For example, pictorial appeals to the saints usually include some sign of the saints within the picture's space, but instances in which no saints or signs appear might be legitimately considered apostrophes.

■ apotropaic

having the power to avert evil or bad fortune, as in a good luck charm or talisman.

■ appeal to precedent

X should be allowed (or not) because some analogous Y has been allowed (or not). This structure of informal logic is very widely used in writing about art, especially in attributions and interpretations, but it is rarely explicitly identified or critiqued on the basis of its logicality.

■ appetitive drive

any of the instinctual urges thought to require some sort of satisfaction of a need, as in hunger, sexuality, sleep, etc. For example, Friedrich Nietzsche and many others have thought that sexual appetite was the real drive behind works of art, even the high idealism of Raphael.

■ apollonian

Friedrich Nietzsche's designation for the calm, conscious, orderly and rational side of human nature.

■ appropriation

more aggressive than allusion or citation, appropriation is the excision of material from one context and its reuse in another context, usually with intent to expose some unrecognised irony in the original or to undermine notions of authorial responsibility.

arbiter elegantiarum

a putative final authority or judge in matters of taste.

archaeology

the scientific study of the material remains of past cultures.

archetypal criticism

usually Jungian, but any criticism which seeks to discover the role of archetypes in generating meaning.

archetype

an essentialist term imported from Jungian analysis, it means basic, unchanging images of a primordially mythic character that reside in the collective unconscious. The presumption is that these images are universal, transcultural and transhistorical.

argument

in informal logic, a propositional form in which premises (reasons) are given in support of a claim (conclusion). While most art is not propositional and therefore cannot be construed as argument in itself, much (if not all) art criticism is implicitly or explicitly a matter of substantiating claims about a work.

argument from analogy

if X is true, Y is likely to be true if it is similar in sufficient, relevant aspects and if it is not relevantly dissimilar.

Aristotelian

pertaining to the thought of Aristotle and his followers.

art

human agency, whether through manual skills (as in the art of sailing or painting or photography), intellectual manipulation (as in the art of politics) or public or personal expression (as in the art of conversation). As such, the word is etymologically related to artificial, i.e., produced by human beings. Since this embraces many types of production that are not conventionally deemed to be art, perhaps a better term would be culture. This would explain why certain preindustrial cultures produce objects which Eurocentric interests characterise as art, even though the producing culture has no linguistic term to differentiate these objects from utilitarian artefacts.

■ art appreciation
the introduction of basic principles of visual literacy, especially the fundamentals of formal analysis without reference to iconography or historical context, to general audiences for the purpose of enhancing their enjoyment of works of art in non- academic contexts. In some postmodernisms, the term has a slightly pejorative tone indicating unreflective indulgence.

■ art conservation
principally, the technical study of the best ways to preserve and protect artworks from physical deterioration. However, some programmes in art conservation also address related issues, such as the ethics of conservation, art restoration, museology and so on.

■ art for art's sake
any of a number of positions related to the possibility of art being autonomous or autotelic. The term is usually used of artists and artwriters of the second half of the nineteenth century. In the twentieth century, the notion has been sharply critiqued by Walter Benjamin, among others.

■ artist
a maker of art.

■ art restoration
the rectification of damage to artworks.

■ art theory
the general study of aesthetics and art, with a particular view to elucidating the nature and purpose of works of art. Art theory has been written by practising artists, critics, historians and professional philosophers. It is impossible

to see a work of art without theory. Although art theory sometimes deals with history and ideology, historical methodologies and postmodernism in general are more directly concerned with and responsive to them.

■ artistic biography

the interpretive mode which seeks to produce an accurate account of an artist's life and/or foregrounds data about an artist's life in the discussion and evaluation of the artwork.

■ arts journalism

the production of descriptive reviews of arts activities (including dance, drama, music, theatre, visual arts, etc.) for publication in the mass media. Because it is usually directed towards a general audience, much arts journalism has not been very critically acute.

■ artwork

a work of art. Sometimes, like oeuvre, it can also signify an entire body of works.

■ artwriter

a practitioner of artwriting.

■ artwriting

the term is more or less a conception of art criticism and art history as essentially rhetorical, rather than scientific, i.e. the primary characteristic of both is persuasive instrumental value, not truth value.

■ aside

a term used mostly in theatre and film criticism to describe the dramatic convention in which an actor directly addresses the audience without the other actors' knowledge.

■ atavism

reversion to an earlier type or to the characteristics of a remote ancestor, as in some varieties of primitivism.

■ a/theology

a unique brand of postmodern theology in which the Bible, God, the self and the Word of traditional theology are mutually interpretable in the terms deriving from deconstruction.

attribute
an object familiarly associated with an office, person or personification, as in the sceptre of a king, the tablets of Moses or the scales of Justice.

attribution
the act of giving credit for an unsigned work to an artist on the basis of similarity of style, iconography or some other material evidence.

audience
originally, a group of listeners. Now, any reader(s), spectator(s) or viewer(s). The traditional distinction between active artists and passive audience is being revised substantially, with much more of the responsibility for meaning going to the latter.

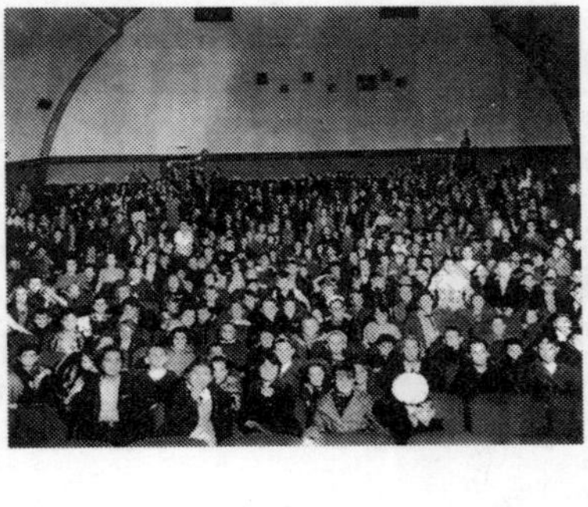

aura
the unique existence of a work of art, its originality and authenticity. Reproduction withers the aura, detaching the object from the domain of tradition and 'liquidating the traditional value of the cultural heritage'.

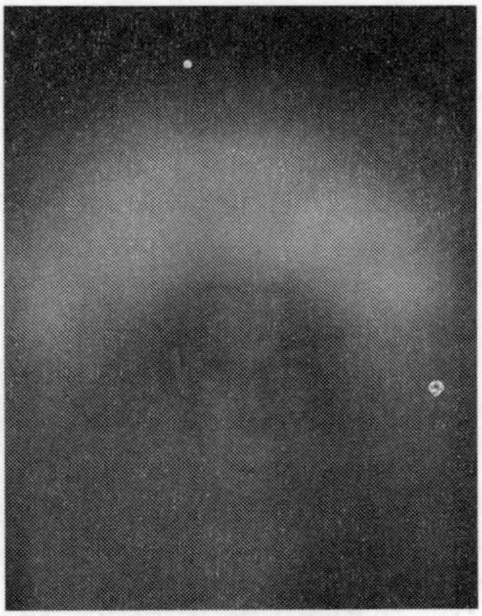

auteur theory
the still fashionable theory that a single filmmaker, almost always the director, is fully and finally responsible for the creative processes that make the finished product.

authenticity
generally, the condition of that which is reliable, trustworthy, real, original, unique.

In existentialism, art sometimes plays a primary role in establishing a sense of unique identity in the face of an absurd, basically meaningless world. The resultant freedom to choose, to fashion a meaning for oneself, instead of simply reacting passively to external circumstances is considered authentic.

■ author

'Artist' can refer generically to practitioners of any number of art forms. Similarly, in some contexts 'author' no longer means strictly an editor or writer, but any creator.

■ authorial ignorance

the notion, at least as old as Plato, that authors do not fully understand what their own works are about.

■ authorial irrelevance

the rejection of an author's biography, social context and/or stated intentions in the interpretation of a work. Postmodernism generally takes the idea as a given.

■ authorial responsibility

like the auteur theory in film studies, the notion that artists have conscious, determinate intentions and thus are solely and fully responsible for their work's success or failure, regardless of the audience.

■ authority

the power to act, command or judge. Expertise, mastery or the one who wields such power.

■ autobiographical art

art produced specifically to exploit, illustrate or record events in the life of the artist and/or art produced to give expression to personal thoughts or to vent feelings peculiar to the artist responsible. Autobiographical art is usually indifferent to public themes, but there are recent instances (particularly among feminist artists) in which the personal becomes political, as it were.

■ autoptic

a thing itself used as evidence.

■ **autotelic**
art that has no goal outside of itself, unlike didactic or moralising work. Audiences incapable of tolerating the portrayal of moral excesses or criminal activities in a work of art have refused to acknowledge the possibility of its autotelic status.

■ **autre**
French for other.

■ **autrui**
French for other people or others in general. The term is occasionally used for alterity.

■ **barbarism**
a mistake in the form of a word or image resulting from the violation of a standard custom. Barbarisms are common in modern art, Picasso's Demoiselles d'Avignon is a noted example and in cases of colonialising primitivism, the barbarism works in two directions. E.g., anatomical distortions appropriated from African artefacts violate European standards of figural representation, while the artists who do the appropriating are often indifferent to the significance of the motif in the original culture, thus violating its norms as well.

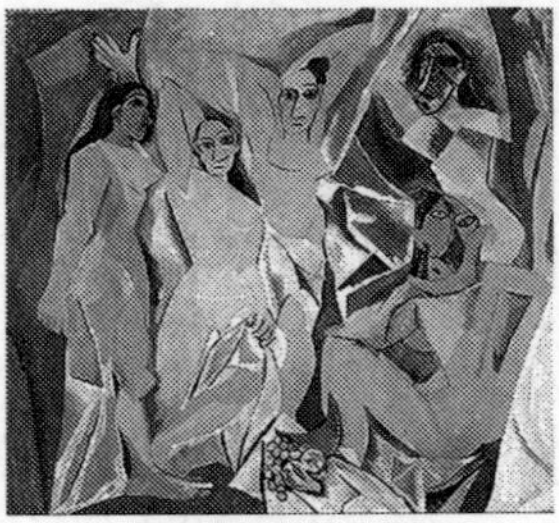

Demoiselles d'avignon

■ **baring the device**
a literary term deriving from Russian formalism, it is what must be done in works of art to show that they are not accurate reflections of reality, as in verisimilitude, but objects unto themselves.

■ **baroque**
once a term of disapprobation, 'baroque' generally means a taste for extravagant forms, often heavy ornamentation and dynamic effects, whether in architecture or in other media. In the seventeenth century, baroque design included classical forms, but it

tended to create an effect of architectural muscularity with repetitions and massings (e.g., of columns on the façade of a building) or by breaking conventions (e.g., breaking a pediment or cornice open, to give it a jagged contour).

■ bassesse

a lowering of a person, state of mind or thing into the primal plane of base materialism. The idea has begun to achieve currency in descriptions of Dionysian works, which generate distaste for some viewers, like those of Mark Prent or Jana Sterbak.

■ beauty myth

title of a controversial book by Naomi Wolf arguing that patriarchal society oppresses women by producing images in fashion, etc., that they cannot emulate without damaging or even destroying themselves.

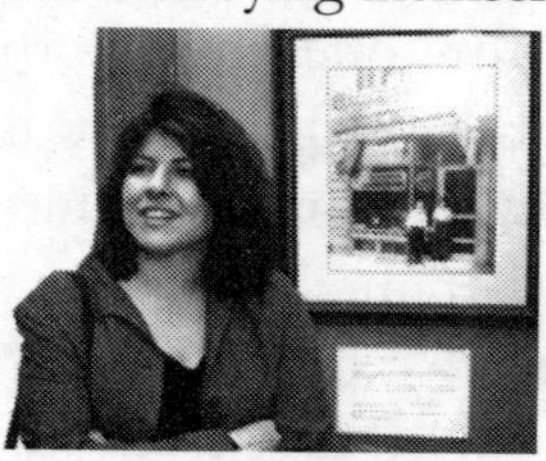

Naomi Wolf

■ behaviour

activity or the combination of observable and describable responses of an agent to internal and external stimuli.

■ betraying versus expressing emotion

in his Principles of Art, R.G. Collingwood ascertained that the simple, unreflective experience of an emotion, with its concomitant distortion of the facial features, etc., was only a matter of betraying emotion.

■ big lie

manipulation of the facts, particularly in popular contexts, to make a story more interesting. For example, some writers think the to-do about political correctness is nothing more than a recent big lie produced within popular culture as part of a decades-old attack on the so-called ivory tower.

■ biographical fallacy

according to formalism and other types of criticism that downplay the role of the author of a work, the erroneous idea that a work's value and meaning reside in the circumstances of the artist's life. It is clear that a psychoanalytical interpretation would also be so understood.

■ biophilic

pertaining to a love of the organic or the natural. Rosa Bonheur and Franz Marc both had strong inclinations of this sort, although they gave them different expressions.

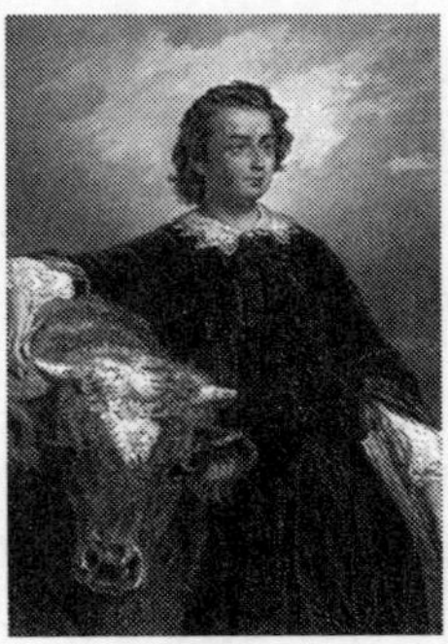

Rosa Bonheur

■ bi-sexism

although the word itself simply means discrimination based on gender, sexism is most often understood as discrimination, specifically against women. That has led Warren Farrell, one of the proponents of the new masculinity, to coin the word 'bi-sexism', to indicate discrimination which works against both males and females.

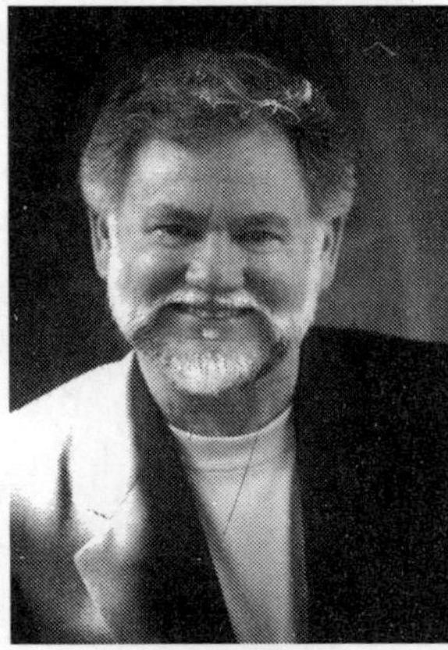

Warren Farrell

■ bistre

a brown wash made from soot, commonly used in the Renaissance.

■ black humour

absurdity, immorality and morbidity used for comic effect or to draw attention obliquely to some regrettable state of affairs that is too painful to confront directly.

■ bodegones

paintings combining genre and still-life, often with a religious scene tucked into the background. Aertsen and

Veláquez painted notable examples.

body colour

a rather opaque type of watercolour, sometimes used sparingly for emphasis and ornament and sometimes used for the entire image, at which point it is likely called a 'gouache'.

bohemianism

deriving ultimately from Gypsy wanderers, thought to have been from Bohemia, Czechoslovakia, Moravia or Romania. Bohemianism evolved into the anti-bourgeois, anti-intellectual, alternative lifestyle of the avant-garde creative community in the Romantic nineteenth century. In the later twentieth century, there are successful artists whose lifestyles are about as far from the marginal as one can get, yet their carefully cultivated cachet of Romantic genius still capitalises on the bohemian myth.

burden of proof

a legal term meaning that the holder of any interpretation diverging from what is objectively describable (i.e., factual) carries the burden of proving that it is plausible beyond a reasonable doubt. Some art criticism, especially subjective impressionism, but by no means only that, seems to have forgotten this basic principle of rational argument.

burlesque

the use of caricature, distortion, exaggeration, irony, parody and/or travesty to ridicule a subject normally treated in a noble or dignified manner.

buttress

any of a variety of structures designed to reinforce a wall, particularly in instances where the thrust of a vault tends to make the walls of a structure spread apart. There are, for example, massive buttresses supporting the giant dome of Hagia Sophia in Istanbul.

caesura

originally the pause in a line of verse, particularly when read aloud. In Painting and Architecture in Italy, Rudolf Wittkower used the word more generally to identify any meaningful break in a pattern, as in a dramatic void in a painting or a formally decisive gap on an architectural facade.

■ caricature

the depiction of exaggerated physical characteristics or personality traits to achieve a burlesque effect. It is most common in drawings and editorial cartoons, but Daumier made several sculptural examples.

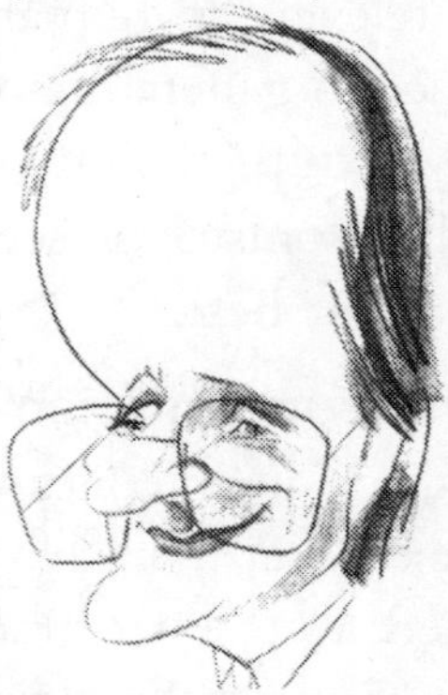

■ carmen figuratum

verbal texts composed so that their printed configuration on the page resembles some aspect of their subject matter. Sometimes also called figure poems.

■ cartesian interactionism

an attempted resolution of the mind-body problem, deriving from René Descartes, which argues that the mind is quite distinct in nature from the body but interacts with it somewhere in the vicinity of the pituitary gland, giving the impression of a unified being.

■ castration

understood as removal of the male sexual organs only, although most standard dictionaries also include something regarding removal of the ovaries. The reason for its inclusion here is the frequency with which this tired idea appears in criticisms influenced by Freudian thought.

■ catechism

religious doctrine put into the set form of questions and answers.

■ categorical statements

in informal logic, statements which pertain to categories or classes of things.

■ categorical syllogisms

in informal logic, three categorical statements related in such a way that two of them, having one term in common, validly yield a third categorical statement relating the remaining two terms. For example, 'All humans are mortal', Michelangelo was human, therefore, Michelangelo was mortal'.

■ category

generally, a class, group or section.

■ catharsis

in Aristotle's poetics, the purgation of the emotions, as if exposure to an affective work of art could cure imbalance of the passions or psychological distress. There has always been debate as to whether this was what Aristotle actually had in mind. In any case, the idea crops up frequently in subsequent expression theory and the like.

■ cathexis

a Freudian term designating the investment of libidinal energy in an idea, image, object or person. Critics fond of discerning appetitive drives in a work of art might be inclined to make use of the concept.

■ causality

the relation of cause and effect.

■ central

in postmodernist critiques, especially, the self-indulgent tendency of one group to see itself as more important, more highly developed or more relevant to human experience in general than any other group, which is ignored, colonised or seen as tributary at best.

■ chameleon criticism

critical acts in an educational context are usually performed at the front of a darkened room by lecturers whose bodies interfere with projected images and thus distort them. Chameleon criticism is a figurative term to indicate the way in which critics hide themselves by taking on the colouring and markings of the object in question. From the point of view of the object or of a hypothetical postmodernist third party, the camouflage can be seen as self-deception on the part of the critics, i.e. the critics fool themselves that they have attained objectivity.

channel

in information theory, a path along which data can be transferred.

character

1. the human beings, anthropomorphised creatures and personifications that serve as actors in drama, image, narrative and the like.
2. the intellectual, moral, psychological and other components of a personality.
3. those aspects of an experience, image, object and the like that give it a particular flavour or quality of experience.

charm

an object or utterance intended to have a magical effect.

chiaroscuro

in conventional artwriting, chiaroscuro means merely modelling a form, as in a shaded drawing, in terms of light and dark. As such, chiaroscuro is a generic term and does not describe a particular manner of modelling.

chiasmus

the inversion of parallel phrases in poetic syntax, as in 'He went to the city, to the country went she' or Keats's 'Beauty is truth, truth beauty'. In Tradition and Desire, Norman Bryson uses the term to characterise a curious inversion of visuality present in images of people in meditation. Whereas Michael Fried (in Absorption and Theatricality) sees paintings of distracted figures as excluding the viewer, Bryson sees them as implying the viewer through chiastic reversal.

chomskyan

pertaining to the theories of linguist Noam Chomsky.

chronocentrism
the self-indulgent tendency of the most recent era (and its history, values, etc.) to see itself as more important, more highly developed or more relevant to human experience in general than any other era.

cinematic
pertaining to devices, usually visual, characteristic of films and filmmaking.

circuit of visualities
Norman Bryson's characterisation of the way visuality circulates in a social context.

circumstantial evidence
demonstrable facts, events or states that condition or determine the inference of another concomitant fact, event or state. This is a legal term, but its applicability to interpretation based on context is clear.

citation
like quotation in a written text, an artist's use of material from another source to contribute to a new image, whether in terms of form or of content. Much of the historical eclecticism in, for example, nineteenth-century architecture consisted of citations.

class logic
that which pertains to categorical statements (relations between classes of things) and categorical syllogisms.

classic, classical
classic means of the highest order or rank, whereas classical means characteristic of Greek and Roman antiquity and things made in emulation thereof. For example, Picasso's Guernica (1937) may well be a classic, but it is hardly classical. That is, it may have a certain staying power in history based on any number of assumptions, including quality, but it does not exhibit any characteristics associated with various classical schools, like rationalism and impersonal execution.

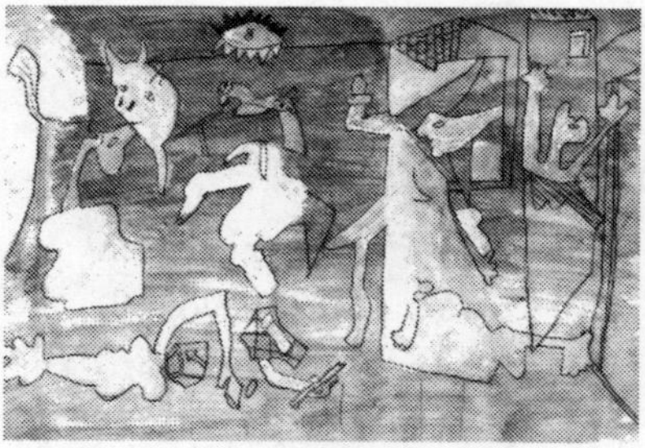

Guernica

■ classism

by analogy with racism and sexism, a disparaging attitude towards members of other social ranks. The word is not to be confused with 'classicism', the veneration of the classical heritage.

■ cliche

an expression that has become hackneyed or trite through overuse or unrecognised banality. There are innumerable examples: the 'poignant' juxtaposition of youth and old age, the clutching of the forehead to indicate intellectuality, etc.

■ climax

in traditional narrative analysis, the dramatic or emotional height in a narrative. E.g., in a hypothetical telling of the story of Medusa, if the crisis were the point at which Perseus finds he cannot avoid confronting the infamous Gorgon, the climax would be the moment he holds her severed head triumphantly aloft.

■ closure

1. in Gestalt perceptual psychology, the satisfaction of a pattern encoded, as it were, into the brain, thus triggering recognition of the stimulus. This can involve the brain's provision of missing details thought to be a part of a potential pattern or, once closure is achieved, the elimination of details unnecessary to establish a pattern match. Both conditions can lead to erroneous interpretations of a stimulus, a famous example of which is the alternating figure.

2. the sense of a definite conclusion, a tying up of all loose ends and a final determinacy of meaning. The possibility of an exhaustive interpretive conclusion extending to all details of a

work with equal validity is challenged by postmodernism in general.

■ code

1. a conventional meaning arbitrarily assigned to a symbol.

2. a set of transformational rules for converting the meanings of one semiotic system into another. Although the term has very specific applications in the work of some critics, it is generically used to indicate the presence of some latent meaning 'behind' a manifest one which must thus be decoded for exposure to the understanding.

■ coextension

an overlapping of sorts, but instead of involving two originally separate things, coextension concerns one thing, which can operate in several ways in different contexts. E.g., an F sharp is the same key on a piano as a G flat, but to identify that note with the former term in the latter's key would introduce contextual distortion.

■ cognates

similar words, in two or more languages, which are related by descent from the same ancestral language. For example, the English 'history' and the French 'histoire' are both descendants from the Latin 'historia'.

■ cognitive

pertaining to the act or processes of knowing and perceiving. Most aesthetic theories argue that art is not a matter of mere decoration because of its various appeals to the various cognitive faculties of the mind.

■ cognitive dissonance

a psychological term denoting the mental state in which two or more incompatible or contradictory ideas, e.g. enjoying smoking and knowing it to be unhealthy, are both held to be true. While a person who is successful at keeping them in suspension might be said to have a high degree of negative capability, implying that the conception has a potentially useful role to play in psychological criticism, a person who is not successful may simply be repressing one of the ideas in favour of the other, thus producing dissonant discomfort.

■ collaboration

a putatively basic paradigm of female acculturation, as opposed to male competition.

■ collage

the gluing together of bits and pieces of originally unrelated images and parts thereof, including previously used commercial materials, to create something unprecedented (rather than in imitation of the world). By analogy, any act of criticism which adopts a similar technique, usually (but not necessarily) relating visual fragments with citations, paraphrases and the like from other critical acts, chiefly as a strategy to avoid determinacy.

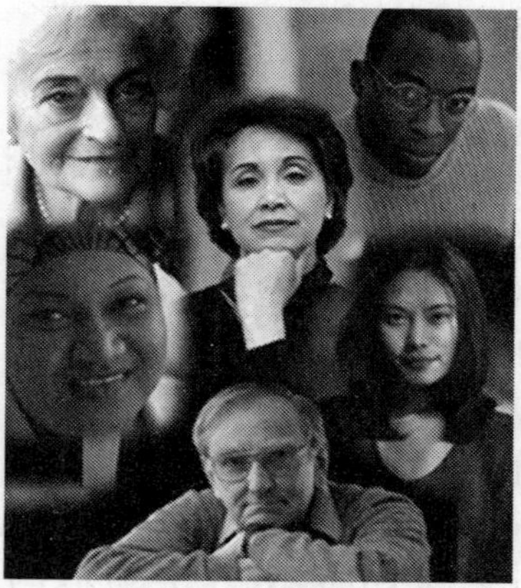

■ collective consciousness

Emil Durkheim's term (in The Rules of Sociological Method) to distinguish how collective representations give shape to personal associations and aspirations in such a manner as to represent a social heritage in a given time and place. As such, the term is a near synonym of horizon of expectations or social formation, with a more sociological and psychological spin.

■ collective representations

distinguishable values and sentiments as they link with shared cultural symbols in a given time and place. Collective representations differ in type and range, from the moral status quo reiterated nightly in television sitcoms to specific symbols of revolt in, say, punk subculture.

■ collective unconscious

the field of inherited ideas, images, legends, myths and the like that exists beyond individual memory but nonetheless informs it. The presumption is that just as biological evolution passes through preliminary stages, which remain as, say, vestigial organs or structures in more developed species, the mind too retains remnants of earlier stages in its development.

■ colloquialism

slang or informal everyday speech. Perhaps, the notion could usefully be applied to the visual arts, to relax some of the tension involved in words like realism and slice-of-life. The notion can also be applied to visual slang.

■ colonialism

the process in which an empowered culture assimilates, destroys or estranges a powerless one. Colonialism differs from imperialism chiefly in the degree of subjugation of the native culture.

■ colourist tradition

in the history of art, there is an imaginary line of development moving from early colourists like the Venetian painters, who ostensibly placed more emphasis on colour than on line, design or concept, to later colourists like the Impressionsists, some of whom went so far in stressing colour over drawing and composition that their works appear quite amorphous, like veils of coloured light.

■ colour

in very formal writing about colour, the word 'colour' refers simply to the broad category of visual phenomena in which one can differentiate objects (even otherwise identical objects) by virtue of differences in the portions of the spectrum of light that they reflect. That is, colour does not mean a particular colour, but the category that includes particular hues and other things like tints, shades, brightness and saturation.

■ **colour temperature**

see **cool colour**, **warm colour**.

■ **combined studies**

the use of more than one more narrowly defined type of criticism or historical methodology. In actual practice, most interpretations are combined studies in some respect.

■ **commedia dell'arte**

a popular form of comedy in 16th-18th century Italy, in which they used improvised dialogue and masked actors in farcical drama, pantomime, song and dance. It engendered some very famous individual characters, most notably Harlequin and Columbine. Its influence on French pantomime and English harlequinade was huge in theatre history and a few artists really capitalised on those characters for their own ends.

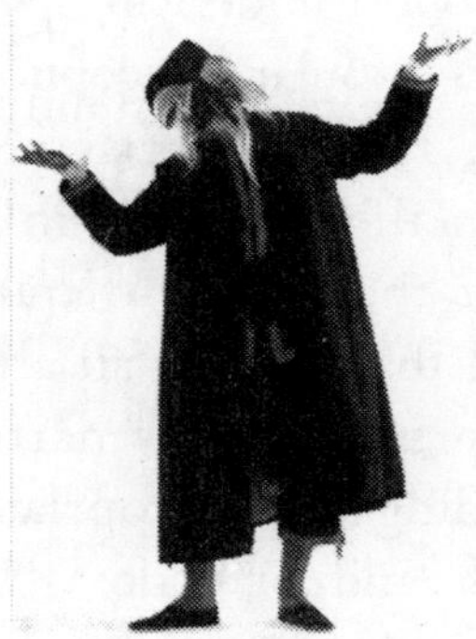

■ **commercial art**

visual art produced principally for commercial purposes such as advertising, as opposed to fine art.

■ **commodity**

an article of commerce. Describing an artwork as a commodity overtly downplays any other function it might have had, like personal expression, communication, propaganda, etc.

■ **common sense**

in postmodernism, in general, common sense is considered a fiction created by those in power to convince the oppressed that ideology is simply the way things really are.

■ **communication**
a notion underlying particularly popular conceptions of art, i.e. that artists have something specific in mind that they want to transmit and that making an artwork is principally a matter of finding an appropriate vehicle and/or code.

■ **communication theory**
another name for information theory.

■ **community**
see **interpretive community**.

■ **compensatory**
counterbalancing, neutralising, making compensation for some injury or lack. The idea is fundamental to many of the principles of psychoanalytic criticism.

■ **competition**
according to Eisler's The Chalice and the Blade, a putatively basic paradigm of male acculturation as opposed to female collaboration or partnership.

■ **complaint**
a literary term indicating the expression of sorrow or lament in fairly fixed form. Some of the more rhetorical paintings of lamentation or bereavement might be so described. A lament, in contrast, is usually more heartfelt.

■ **complementary colours**
see **primary colours**.

■ **complication**
in a narrative, the development of the opposing forces set in motion by the conflict. Sometimes also called the rising action.

■ **conceit**
a striking image, motif or theme, often an elaborate or even fanciful controlling metaphor. Strong conceits were particularly common in Italian Baroque art (e.g., Bernini's additions to St. Peter's as ecclesia triumphans).

■ concept

1. familiarly, something conceived in the mind, as in a thought or notion, especially when it concerns generalisation from particular instances.

2. more specifically, the mathematician Gottlob Frege defined 'concept' as an incomplete predicate, which can achieve reference only with the addition of some other component.

■ conceptual

pertaining to concepts. More specifically, art possessing imagery that departs from perceptual accuracy to present a conception of the object, rather than its appearance alone. It has become fairly standard, for example to characterise the rigidly formal art of ancient Egypt as conceptual, whereas Courbet's Realism is perceptual.

■ concetto

a conceit. The plural is concetti.

■ concrete

particular, real, tangible.

■ concrete poetry

poetry in which layout and typography play visual roles. Including paralinguistic inflection as well as resemblance, the term's use is slightly more general than carmen figuratum, which is more likely to resemble what it describes.

■ concrete universal

the expression in the particular here and now of some putatively universal essence. Hegel illustrated the idea with the concept of law, which supposedly arises from the will of the people, rather than from an individual. In that respect, law is universal, but since the people are bound by time and space, their law is concrete. Structurally similar arguments for the timelessness of art are made all the time. The notion is very common in classical schools of thought, but it is frequently frowned upon by postmodernists.

condensation

a basic psychological process described in Freud's Interpretation of Dreams and elsewhere whereby the dreaming mind, unable to express its desires literally because of some psychic blockage or social restriction, finds a way to do so figuratively by compressing several latent elements into one manifest one.

conditional fallacies

the invalid reverse of the conditional inferences, i.e., denying the antecedent and affirming the consequent. For example, 'If Cindy Sherman is late for the meeting, (then) Jenny Holzer will be angry; Jenny Holzer is angry, so Cindy Sherman is late for the meeting'. Jenny Holzer could be angry for some other, unstated reason, so this argument fallaciously affirms the consequent.

confession

a literary term describing a type of autobiography, but one which is more private and personal in nature. The concept could be used to describe works ranging from Dürer's famous nude self-portrait to some of the more self-conscious productions of the Surrealists.

configuration

a form or figure, as in Gestalt.

confabulation

a psychological term denoting a compensation for memory loss by the invention of fictitious details.

conflation

a fusion, confusion or combination of elements into a composite whole.

conflict

tension in general. In narrative analysis, the opposition of forces that gives momentum to a narrative.

connaissance

Lacanian term for knowledge within the imaginary.

connoisseur

generally, a person of refined sensibility and discriminating taste. More specifically, as initiated by Charles Eastlake in the early nineteenth century, one who professes to know, from the Latin cognoscere, about such matters.

connoisseurship

in the 1870s, Giovanni Morelli took the notion of the connoisseur and added to it a quasi-scientific method to make attributions of works of art by paying special attention to marginal details. Assuming that specific connoisseurs were genuinely in possession of special knowledge, they could identify artists with an authoritative discrimination that all but escaped the run-of-the-mill viewer. Since then, connoisseurship has implied secure standards of judgement. Although connoisseurship is a perfectly legitimate method within art history, its occasional tendencies towards pretentiousness have become a favourite target of popular writers and the media in general.

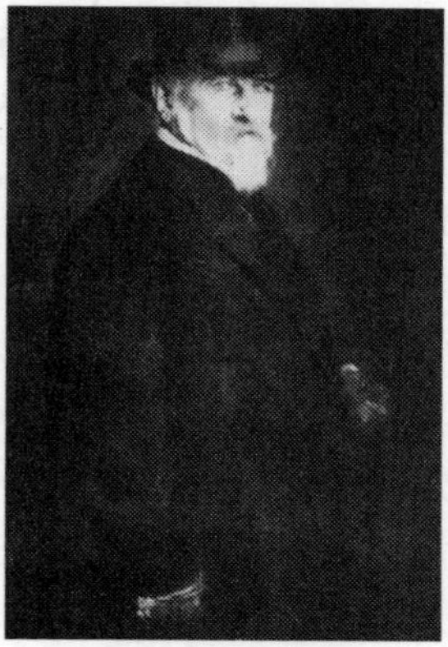

Giovanni Morelli

connotations

figurative meanings, emotional baggage and conventional associations accruing to words and images, as opposed to their literal meanings or denotations. Connotations may be universal, restricted to a group (e.g., a nationality or a social class) or personal. The usefulness of the latter category is questionable, since it is quite possible for an individual viewer to read into a work personal connotations which are not shared by a general audience.

consciousness

standard works on psychology will break this into two basic categories:

1. the state of awareness.
2. the subjective aspect of neurological activity. There are subcategories and variations of these. For example, some define consciousness as the totality of experience at any given instant, as opposed to 'mind', which is the sum of all past moments of consciousness. The term has slightly different connotations in the philosophy of mind.

constant conjunction

David Hume denied that certain events caused others in strictly definable ways derived from empirical observation. Instead, he asserted that what appeared to be causality was simply the result of mental habits that saw apparent causes and apparent effects as constantly conjoined, whether or not they really had anything to do with one another.

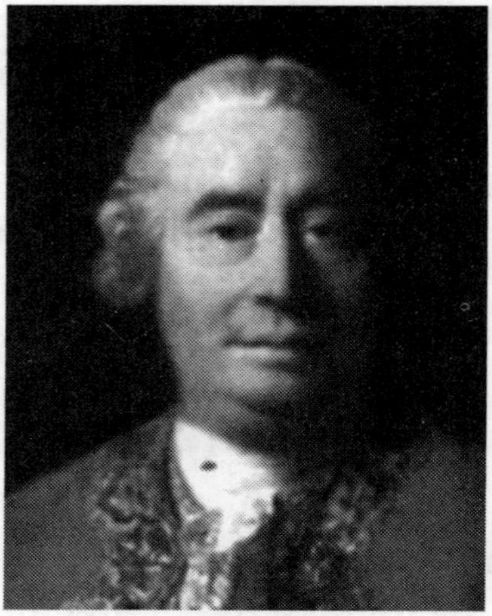

David Hume

constative

an utterance that describes a condition, fact or state of affairs and can thus be judged as true or false.

constellation

a cluster of ideas held together by some common term or idea or merely by association. A psychoanalytical constellation, for example, is a group of unrepressed, emotionally loaded thoughts or impressions. In semantics, a constellation is a cluster of possibilities in meaning which, under normal circumstances, is filtered in such a way as to produce a meaningful effect.

■ constitutive
having the power to create, enact, establish. The word's most frequent use in contemporary artwriting is in Marxist and Foucauldian contexts, especially where a meaning or even an artwork itself is described as without objective, independent existence but has the appearance of it because of the way it is constituted by an act of criticism or an institutional framework in which, for example, one thing is recognised as another thing.

■ construct
fashionable term indicating something constructed by mental effort or more particularly, through political and social mechanisms.

■ consummatory field
in The Work of Art, Stephen Pepper argues that viewers have an appetitive drive which requires them to examine a work of art in the best (or optimum) position for satisfaction or consummation. Characteristics of the artwork itself determine that optimum position. A simple example might be a painting in linear perspective, which demands that a viewer physically occupy a given position for the image to appear in correct proportion. Viewers will typically explore possible positions, which really need not be just physical points in space, until they find the correct one that satisfies their drive, relative to the artwork at hand. Their explorations are said to take place in a consummatory field.

■ content
there is no clear consensus on what the content of a work of art is. Some would distinguish subject matter from content, i.e. denotations vs. connotations, more or less, while others would prefer terms like meaning and significance. What follows is a provisional record which tries to take into account most of the available possibilities. For the sake of

categorical clarity, we can arbitrarily differentiate content from form and context, although there are clear points of interchange or mutual inflection. Simply put, content is 'what' the work is (about), while form and context are 'how' the work is and 'in what circumstances' the work is, respectively.

■ **context**
context means the varied circumstances in which a work of art is (or was) produced and/or interpreted.

■ **contextualism**
more or less a synonym of relativism.

■ **contingency**
dependence on accident, chance, possibility, uncertainty or other non-essential factors. A certain degree of contingency is necessary if productive dialogism is to take place.

■ **contrast**
generally, the exhibition of difference or juxtaposition of dissimilar elements in a work of art, as in the contrast of colours, textures and what have you.

■ **controlling image**
the basic image or metaphor that informs a more complicated sequence and gives it the unity of purpose. Controlling images are frequently used in religious art (e.g., the Stations of the Cross, Michelangelo's Neoplatonism, Bernini's conceit of ecclesia triumphans) and in movements of pronounced Romantic sensibility (e.g., Max Klinger's glove, Max Ernst's femme sans tête).

■ **controlling metaphor**
see **controlling image**.

■ **convention**
an agreement, custom, formality, standard interpretation or practice and the like.

■ **conventional**
pertaining to conventions. Certain images have purely conventional, figurative meanings, many of which seem to have been forgotten in popular culture. One such

is a child blowing bubbles, which is a vanitas.

convergers and divergers

in Contrary Imaginations, Liam Hudson postulated two personality types with respect to the way they achieve goals. Some do so in a direct, linear fashion, as it were, proceeding from the general to the particular by a process of elimination and by establishing causal relationships. They are said to converge on their goal. Others approach a problem in a more open-ended manner, as if they expand their investigation across a field of possibilities, thus diverging. The terms lend themselves to distinctions between scientific and artistic personalities, as well as to the difference between vertical and lateral thinking.

conversational style

differences in verbal expression arising from gender, socialisation and other factors, including ethnic origins, class associations, etc. The idea provides some interesting material for speculation regarding analogous differences in art produced by men and women, different ethnic and social groups and so on.

cool colour

blue and the admixtures of it and the other primary colours, like greens and violets, are conventionally referred to as cool colours, ostensibly by virtue of their resemblance to the natural hue of water, grass and other cool things. Cool colours are said to recede or retreat, i.e., to draw towards the background of an image and so are said to be generally opposed to the temperature and movement of warm colour. The effect can be both visual and symbolic.

co-opt

to absorb or assimilate. The notion is particularly important in discussions of modernism and postmodernism. Modernism, for example, is said to have fancied itself perennially outside mainstream culture in order to critique it from the position of the avant-garde. Of course, the institutions of the artworld have co-opted modernism so that the avant-garde is mainstream culture. There are similar issues in postmodernism, but one of the more important ones is raised under the heading parody.

■ correlation

interdependency, mutual relationship, simultaneous occurrence and the like. Correlation is not necessarily an indicator of causality, as a recent book entitled innumeracy points out. A positivist science of interpretation would want to distinguish very clearly between the two in order to be sure that feature 'X' in a work of art was genuinely produced by factor 'Y' in the context, instead of simply accompanying it.

■ correlational social histories

a species of artwriting that gives priority to secondary context without necessarily distinguishing between causality and correlation in the formation of the work's content. Examples include economic developments that encouraged Venetian landowners to build inland, thus affecting the career of Palladio (James Ackerman).

■ correspondence theory of truth

in philosophy, the theory that statements are true to the extent that they actually describe some state of affairs in the real world. In Tenured Radicals, Roger Kimball attacks the cultural left, saying that it rejects the correspondence theory of truth on the grounds that there is no objective reality for any statements to correspond to.

■ counter-intuitive

running against unreflective expectations. Some archaeologists, for example, have recently discovered that paper biodegrades much more slowly and that disposable diapers take up much less space than is generally thought. The 'intuitive' in the phrase thus relates directly to the ideological effect. Art criticism often entails a certain counter-intuition, for what an artwork first seems to mean is frequently not what it ends up meaning. A healthy critical attitude in nearly every academic discipline almost always entails patience, a refusal to jump to conclusions and an openness to the counter-intuitive.

■ counterpart

English translation of Lacanian use of 'semblable', to describe the specular ego developed during the mirror stage.

■ counterpoint

a musical term meaning the interplay of parts against one another, as it were, to enliven by continuous contrasts, tensions and resolutions. In the visual arts, it usually applies to smaller, formal components of an image, rather than to larger, more monumental tensions. As far as theory and interpretation are concerned, the notion is subsumed by dialectic, although some of the multivocal passages in Derrida's The Truth in Painting are more happily described as contrapuntal.

■ counterspeech

in 'The Value of the Canon', Irving Howe said a canon was useful not as something simply to be memorised, obeyed or worshipped but as an opportunity to practice what Robert Frost called 'couterspeech', an active engagement with the products of other minds and voices with which we might not agree. The value of the canon is thus literally as material for the development of a skill, rather than indoctrination. Counterspeech might thus be thought of as a conservative version of dialogism.

craft
since the Renaissance fine art has distinguished itself from craft in the conventional sense of 'mere' manual dexterity or technical skill. In the era of mechanical reproduction, of course, this notion of craft has generally suffered a loss of respect. On the other hand, certain recent developments, like the flourishing of ceramics programs and feminist reclamations of women's crafts have counterbalanced the trend.

credulity
the opposite of scepticism, an uncritical acceptance of undemonstrable assertions.

crisis
in narratology, the point at which a narrative is most likely to change its apparent direction or momentum. The term is not synonymous with climax.

critic
one who analyses, evaluates or expresses an opinion on a work of art, from a cluster of Greek words meaning to decide, to discern, to judge.

critical idealism
synonym for 'transcendental idealism'.

critical theory
a specific range of Marxist approaches common among the members of the Frankfurt School, thus not to be confused with the generic phrases 'theories that are critical' or 'theories about criticism'. Critical theory rejects positivism and value-freedom in science and dogma in Marxism, advocating instead an open-ended, continuously self-critical process that will eventually contribute to social reform.

critical thinking
within the framework of scepticism, critical thinking is synonymous with informal logic. The standards for what is considered critical thinking in many other contexts can be less rigorous and should be examined carefully on a case by case basis.

criticism
the analysis, evaluation, interpretation and study of works of art. While it is certainly true that disapproving remarks are sometimes made, it is a common mistake to assume that 'criticism' simply means negative commentary and that to be critical means to be cynical, derogatory and insulting. While there is a multitude of critical methods, it is the contention of this glossary that their bewildering variety is created by subtle adjustments, selective foregroundings and interplays of the subdivisions of three basic structural elements: form, content and context, i.e. critical methodologies as diverse as connoisseurship and structuralism, are related in that they both address formal aspects of works of art.

critique
an instance of serious practical criticism. The term is also habitually used of the evaluation of fine arts students' work, but the intellectual level of these critiques varies widely from instructor to instructor and institution to institution.

critique of institutions
any critique addressing the constitutive role of a social institution, whether it be a governmental body, a horizon of expectations, a curatorial policy or whatever. Mainstream art magazines, for example, in a sense create the work they supposedly describe because they are imbricated in a commercial network of sales and advertising strategies.

critique of representation
term used with increasing frequency in postmodernism to challenge a number of the conventional assumptions of art as communication among other things.

cross-cutting
a film term indicating the sequential presentation of actions understood to be contemporaneous or in rapid succession. Its usefulness in static visual art is limited to

suites of images, like comic books, a few collections of prints and the few collage-novels produced by the Surrealists.

■ cultural analysis

a loosely employed term, but one which usually indicates a serious, multidisciplinary, critical approach to cultural phenomena in a variety of media, frequently with a view to exposing unarticulated social norms. As such, it has certain similarities with the much older Geistesgeschichte school of thought. There is, however, a much greater stress on popular culture, especially from a semiotic point of view.

■ cultural anthropology

anthropology that deals with cultural practices in a multidisciplinary manner, drawing on archaeology, ethology, ethnography and linguistics, among others.

■ cultural democracy

occasionally used as a near synonym of multiculturalism. It is thus not to be confused with 'democratisation of culture', which simply means 'bringing culture to the masses'.

■ cultural left

vaguely defined, usually journalistic conception of the anti-traditional proponents of multiculturalism and/or political correctness as heirs to the radical politics of the 1960s, especially feminism and Marxism and supposedly related tendencies, like deconstruction and ethnicity.

■ culture

for some it means high art and only high art, as in Matthew Arnold's shopworn phrase 'the best that has been thought and said in the world'. In other more anthropological applications, it has a hypothetical standard of excellence than a generalised 'way of life, which expresses certain meanings and values not only in art and learning, but also in institutions and ordinary behaviour.' In most postmodernism contexts, the latter connotation is the more common. If we understand nature as the world and its phenomena as they exist without human intervention, then 'culture' means all things produced by human agency: decorative artefacts, environmental pollutants, high art, political ideologies, ritual beliefs, social customs and so on.

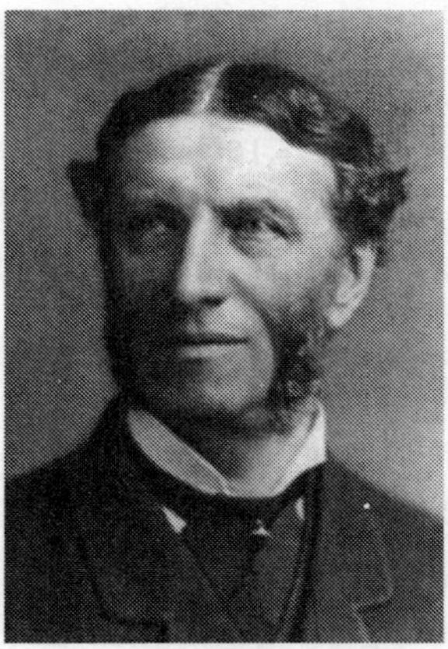

Matthew Arnold

culture jamming

a colloquialism referring to a species of media activism usually presented in the form of a fraudulent mass media event. One of the larger organizations dedicated to culture jamming, especially in the form of advertising parodies, is Adbusters, which publishes in Vancouver, B.C., a magazine which reaches an international readership.

cumulative impression

a simple way of illustrating the hermeneutic circle, even as it avoids the closure thus produced. When audiences encounter a work of art for the first time, they will get a first impression of what it is about. Perhaps, when they learn something specific about the artist, their interpretations will veer in the direction of artistic biography. Or, if they learned that the work was for a powerful patron, the interpretation would veer towards one of the correlational social histories in a modest form. Similarly, any responses communicated to them, even ones that are totally irresponsible subjective impressionism, will also add to the process.

dasein

literally 'being there', Dasein is Heidegger's term for the manner in which beings relate themselves to the world around them, but from which they are existentially alienated. Dasein is divided into three modes of possible existence: factuality, existentiality and fallenness. The first of these needs no explanation. The second refers to the state in which beings achieve knowledge of their purpose in life and the resultant authenticity. The third refers to the inauthentic existence of those who do not realise their purpose. The usefulness of art in this scheme is a function of the drive towards existentiality.

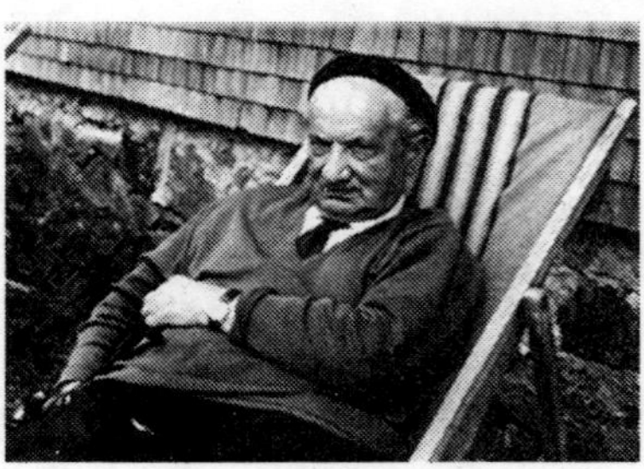

Heidegger

■ date stamp

Freud's analogy between daydreaming and poetic invention did not presuppose that a given fantasy always had the same latent meaning. Instead, it could be marked with a date-stamp of sorts, which would indicate the current impressionism to which the fantasy was linked. In the past or the future, the same manifest fantasy could have some other significance altogether.

■ dead metaphor

a metaphorical cliché, which, through age or frequency of use, is understood as literal, with its figurative level forgotten or unrecognised. The history of art is riddled with dead metaphors. The average viewer rarely thinks of the vanitas theme when regarding a still life and the photographs of authors on book-jackets frequently exploit poses derived from standard portrayals of ancient philosophers.

■ death of the author

the term derives from an essay by that name in Roland Barthes' celebrated Image Music Text, where he presented the notion of a text as something without a fixed meaning apart from that produced by readers in the act of reading.

■ decoding
the discovery of latent meaning behind manifest meaning.

■ decorum
an academic principle that a given subject should be presented in a suitable style. E.g., noble figures should be presented with a dignified mien in stable compositions, while revellers can be depicted in more dynamic settings.

■ deduction
a valid argument in which one cannot assert the premises and deny the conclusion without violating the laws of thought, particularly that of non-contradiction. For example, in the categorical syllogism: 'All humans are mortal, Michelangelo was human, therefore, Michelangelo was mortal', one cannot deny Michelangelo's mortality without contradicting one or the other premises.

■ deep structure
see **deep structure and surface structure.**

■ deep structure and surface structure
a basic problem in linguistics is how speakers can recognise meaning in utterances which they have never heard before and how they can recognise identical meanings in different structures (e.g., 'Bonheur painted this picture' and 'This picture was painted by Bonheur'). The Chomskyan answer is that all competent speakers have an innate understanding of a finite set of abstract rules, which determine all basic structural relationships. Combining this deep structure with a set of transformation rules and any new information, allows the speaker to produce new surface structures (i.e., sentences which can be understood even though they contain information which is entirely new to the listener).

■ defamiliarisation
according to Russian literary formalism, defamiliarisation is a key device with which art

prevents us from simply indulging in mental habits. It does this by refusing verisimilitude, drawing attention instead to alienated or estranged aspects of a thing, which closure causes us to overlook or suppress.

■ deficiency

disadvantage, loss and the like. The term is used frequently in neurology, where it might offer an analogy to certain types of deficiency in interpretation.

■ definition

see **definitional rules**.

■ definitional rules

in informal logic, those rules which enable one to determine meaning. It is presumed that a competent speaker will (a) specify the essential characteristics and/or indispensable traits of the thing being defined, (b) will provide sufficient material, i.e. will include neither more nor less than the term being defined and (c) will avoid emotive load. E.g., as a definition, 'Abortion is murder' is insufficient (b) because it tells us nothing about the characteristics of abortion (a) and it is clearly emotively loaded (c). Though nothing is certain, the best way to prepare a definition is through genus and differentia, i.e. to identify the class of things to which the object belongs and then to characterise meaningful differences between it and other members of its class.

■ definitions of art

Ellen Dissanayake's 'What is Art For?' tries to avoid partisanship by simply listing the various ways art has been understood through history: (in no particular order) the product of conscious intention, self rewarding activity, a tendency to unite dissimilar things, a concern with change and variety, aesthetic exploitation of familiarity and surprise or tension and release, the imposition of order on disorder, the creation of illusions, indulgence in sensuousness, the exhibition of skill, a desire to convey meanings, indulgence in fantasy, aggrandisement of self or others, illustration, the heightening of existence, revelation, personal adornment or embellishment and so on.

deictic

a word which shows or points out directly another part of the statement in which it occurs.

deixis

see **deictic**.

déja lu

French play on the phrase 'déja vu' meaning what is described under the heading always-already-read.

déja vu

the illusion of familiarity in a strange place or the feeling of having 'already seen' something which one is supposedly encountering for the first time. The idea has been extended into the act of interpretation as the always-already-read.

deliberative

Aristotelian term for that type of rhetoric used chiefly to persuade an audience.

demagogue

anyone who uses false claims, fallacious reasoning or cultural prejudices in a bid, for fame or power.

demotic

Northrop Frye's term for the style of ordinary speech, as opposed to conventionalised hieratic style. The term has potential usefulness in discussions of folk culture, popular artefacts and the putatively high art influenced by them.

demystification

removal of the mystery, rendering less obscure or decoding. In post-modern contexts, the term has a spin that ranges from correction of social injustice to empowerment of those who have been traditionally suppressed.

demythologise

near synonym of demystify.

denaturalise
to deconstruct familiar notions which we take for granted or unreflectively consider 'normal' or 'natural'. This is a basic procedure in much postmodernism.

denotation
the literal meaning of a word, as opposed to its connotations.

dépense
basically, a Bataillean term for expenditure.

depoliticise
when one discusses an artwork or any other thing without reference to the political and social circumstances informing its creation, one depoliticises it. This is a particular problem when the artwriter's only concern is aesthetics.

depth psychology
the scientific study of human behaviour as the result of largely unconscious processes, as in Freudian and Jungian thought.

Derridean
pertaining to the ideas of Jacques Derrida.

description
discourse intended primarily to produce a mental image of something experienced, as opposed to explaining it.

desire
an urge towards the acquisition of some object (or experience) that appears to promise satisfaction of the urge or enjoyment in general. The role of desire in the creation of art and in supposedly objective artwriting has been under investigation since at least the time of Nietzsche, who asserted that unfulfilled desire was behind the creation of even the virtuous Madonnas of Raphael.

destabilise
a near synonym of denaturalise, with additional spin in the direction of active dismantling of oppressive institutions like canons.

■ **desublimation**

Herbert Marcuse's once influential The Aesthetic Dimension argues that aesthetic form allows a given (social) reality (or the reification thereof) to be sublimated and thus transcended. In turn, this process engenders, in an audience, a rebellious subjectivity, a desublimation of the audience's perceptions, creating a potential indictment of the dominant ideology. Art is thus a dissenting force.

■ **determinacy**

the state of having defined limits or of having such an unequivocal, irreducible meaning that all objective members of an audience will come to the same conclusion, regardless of the differences between their emotional responses.

■ **determinant**

a cause. Determinants may be further described as organismic, environmental or situational to indicate where the determinant comes from: the organism itself, its environment or some antecedent condition that stimulates behaviour. These terms, derived from psychology, are clearly analogous to the subcategories of context.

■ **determinate**

having set limits, established and definitely settled.

■ **determinism**

any of a number of beliefs, both religious and philosophical, that behaviour is predestined or driven by antecedent causes to such a degree that free will is largely an illusion.

■ **detournement**

sometimes translated as 'diversion', which has unfortunate connotations, détournement is the process of turning something aside from its normal course or purpose in an artistic context. While it is typically used as near-synonym of assemblage or collage in a Situationist context, it also describes any process of reinvention, reuse or reinscription of meaning. As a result, outside of Situationist contexts, détournement means any move from the literal to the figurative.

■ **developmental psychology**

the branch of psychology, which studies the growth and maturation of human behaviour, theoretically at all stage of life.

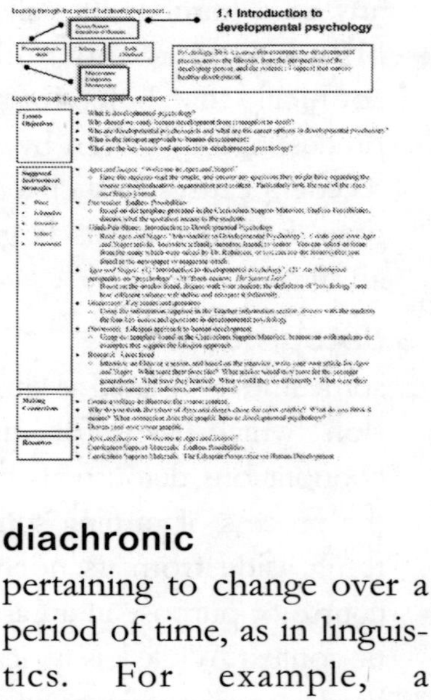

■ **diachronic**

pertaining to change over a period of time, as in linguistics. For example, a diachronic art history is one which follows developments from decade to decade or century to century. In contrast, a synchronic study would examine the constellation of events surrounding a given object of study (i.e., context), ignoring antecedents and consequences.

■ **dialect**

a regional variety of a language, distinguished by accent, grammar, pronunciation, and/or vocabulary. Not to be confused with dialectic or dialogism.

■ **dialectical materialism**

in Marxist thought, dialectical materialism was conceived by Friedrich Engels as an extension of the principles of historical materialism beyond historical and social circumstances into human thought.

■ **dichotomy**

division into two, especially in matters of classification, although many use it as if it were an exact synonym of binary oppositions. The latter, however, entails polar opposites, whereas the former does not have to.

■ didacticism

any practice the principal motivation of which is to teach. It might be useful to ask oneself if the purpose of a particular critique is to make a description, an interpretation or a didactic message. If it is the latter, it might further be useful to ask if the message is that of the work (as in, say, environmentally conscious art) or of the critic.

■ diegesis

an old term for an utterance, in whatever form (descriptions, narratives, propositions, etc.) that makes no evaluation and draws no conclusion.

■ difference

contrast, dissimilarity, distinction, variability, etc. The term is important in postmodern thought for two specific reasons: first, it is a central concept in Saussurean linguistics — Saussure's most quotable quote is 'in language there are only differences without positive terms' — and second, it represents that which androcentrism, Eurocentrism and so on fail to recognise — i.e., the possibility of the other to whom the 'norm' does not apply. E.g., men oppress women because men fail to recognise sexual difference.

■ differentia

see **definitional rules**.

■ difficulty

adversity, complication, inconvenience, obstacle, etc. Once considered completely undesirable, since George Steiner's On Difficulty and Other Essays, it has been seen as appropriate in certain literary contexts, chiefly for the generation of a sense of involvement, even complicity, in the audience.

■ dionysian

Friedrich Nietzsche's designation for the disorderly, irrational, orgiastic and unconscious side of human nature.

■ diptych

two vertical panels hinged together in the centre. Ivory

carvings with religious motifs so arranged were common in late Roman times, as were panels with Christ facing his mother in the late medieval era.

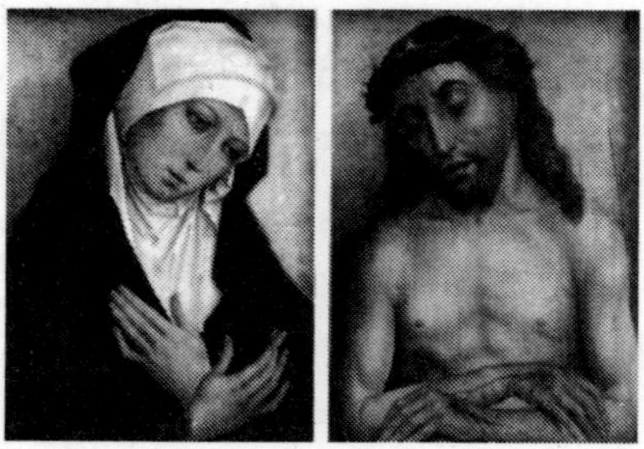

■ **discourse**

generally, a discussion or conversation. More specifically, a mode of expression, originally verbal, but now applied by analogy to other forms. In postmodernism, a discourse is usually the manner of discussion peculiar to a political party, a profession, a scientific method and/or a social group. In other words, discourse is not an absolute, but a relative term which means 'the language with which this particular group describes (evaluates, etc.) its conception of truth as seen through a particular ideology'.

■ **discovery**

1. the exposure of unknown facts to change the unfolding of events in a narrative.
2. a legal term indicating the systematic gathering and exposure of the facts about a case. The systematic nature of the procedure should be emulated in verifiability, although it rarely is, except in the works of particularly thorough.

■ **discursive**

this means both 'pertaining to digression' and 'pertaining to discourse'. It can thus mean either meandering thought or analytical reasoning. 'Discursive thought' usually means propositional thinking in contrast to feelings or unreflective thought driven by emotion.

■ **discursive activity**

Timothy J. Reiss's Discourse of Modernism argues that discursive activity, the flexible, complex and contextually-relative conceptual processes involved in the writing and reading of a text, has been suppressed by what he calls 'analytico-referential' discourse, a dominant cultural model of putative objectivity and realism.

■ disfiguring

title of a 1992 book by a theologian Mark C. Taylor concerning a postmodern aesthetic strategy that involves radically refiguring and disfiguring modernist works, in order to point to their absence of secure signification. Taylor discusses numerous artists and architects in this regard, but his real motive is to expose an unnameable aporia which represents God in some inexplicable way.

■ disinterestedness

impartiality, objectivity, a lack of bias and the like. Not to be confused with a lack of interest, disinterestedness implies that an investigator has no personal interest in whether the result of, say, an experiment turns out to be true or false. Whether it is due to a general tendency towards anti-authoritarian positions or a distant recognition of the indeterminism of quantum mechanics, postmodern thought is usually suspicious of disinterestedness for reasons given under subject presumed to know.

■ displacement

the removal of something from its normal position and/or its replacement. There are three variations on the idea in contemporary discourses. First, Freud saw it as one of the basic processes of dream-work, in which, say, an intolerable desire is displaced from the literal to a figurative expression. For example, a desire to kill one's father might be displaced into a dream of insulting him or doing him less drastic harm. This sense of displacement is still used in psychoanalytical criticism. Developing from this is the second variation, displacement as the psychic origin of metonymy. A third variation is the cultural displacement suggested by Edward Said, in which one culture projects what it is unwilling to recognise in itself onto another, 'lesser' culture.

■ disruption

any of a variety of approaches designed to forestall closure and maintain open-endedness.

■ dissemination

dispersion, derived from the sowing of seeds. Derrida has made special use of the term, punning on semen (seed) and sema (sign) to evoke the idea that signification is a relatively loose scattering of seed/signs, rather than a determinate endeavour. Linking sema to dissemination is, of course, a species of folk etymology.

■ divine afflatus

poetic inspiration of an ecstatic sort. The idea was taken very seriously from Plato onward, but postmodernism generally regards it disdainfully, for reasons analogous to those under the heading genius.

■ doctrinaire

ruled by rigid principle, dogmatic, unreasonably adherent to the canon, biased, narrow-minded and the like.

■ documentary art

any artwork (particularly documentary film and documentary novels) the purpose of which is to record and/or comment on some content, often political or social, by accumulating factual detail.

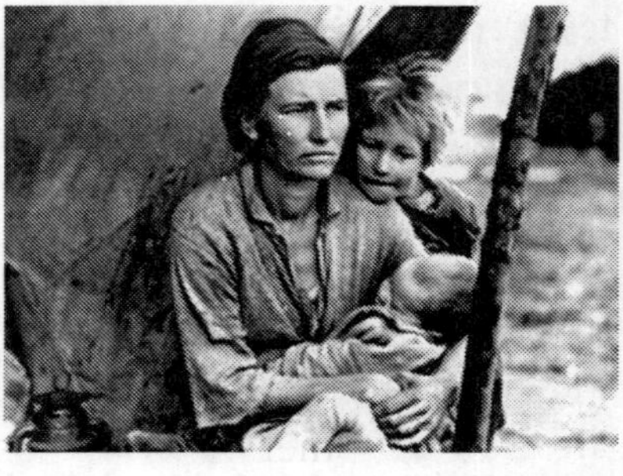

■ dogma

beliefs held to be true and beyond question or debate. Originally the term meant religious truth, but it is now mostly used as a pejorative.

■ dome

a vault, usually with a circular plan and approaching a hemispherical shape, as if one spun an arch three hundred and eighty degrees about its centre.

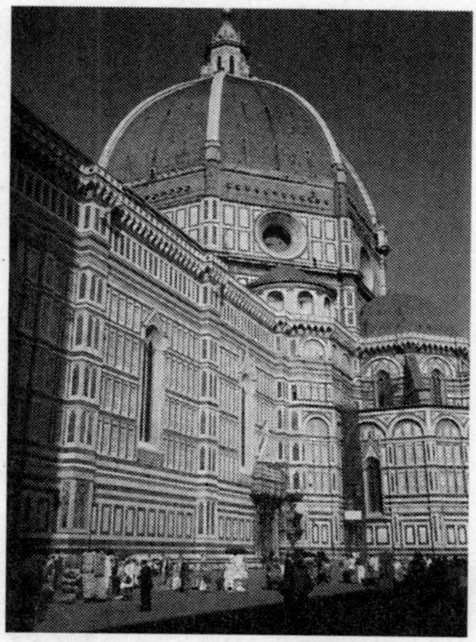

■ dominance

ascendancy, centrality, forcefulness, power, priority, a higher (or the highest) stage in the social hierarchy.

■ dompte-regard

literally, 'tame-gaze'. Jacques Lacan invented the phrase to describe how his conception of a picture functions psychologically.

■ donnée

the given. Henry James introduced the term to indicate the raw material, by analogy with raw data in science, with which any author must start. The presumption is that a donnée is a fact. Some writers seem to present as given instances of folk etymology and sheer confabulations.

■ double articulation

in linguistics, one of the principle characteristics of most languages is a two-fold structure, the first being the level at which phonemes (sounds meaningless in themselves) are brought together into morphemes (arrangements of sounds into the small meaning-bearing components of words) and the second being the syntactic level at which relations between words are produced. One of the problems facing early attempts at a visual semiotics was whether or not visual language possessed a true double articulation.

double entendre
the reverse of a pun. Where a pun is a play on different words with the same sound, a double entendre is a play on a single word with two or more meanings. Double entendres usually have a suggestive or off-colour connotation.

dramatic convention
in the theatre, conventions representing real details that would be too difficult or costly to produce onstage or simply as shorthand devices to propel the narrative forward. The audience recognises these details as conventions but suspends its disbelief.

dramatic irony
ironic meanings recognised by an audience but unrecognised by one or more of the characters in a narrative. This is standard fare in television sitcoms, with the audience laughing at the witlessness of one character or another. In art, the term could be applied to examples ranging from Caravaggio's various Cardsharps and Fortune Tellers to Margaret Bourke-White's At the Time of the Louisiana Flood.

dramatic monologue
originally, a poem in which one speaker addresses a silent listener in terms calculated to give insight into the speaker's experience and spirit.

dramatic propriety
a type of decorum in which an action, a thing or an utterance is judged only by whether it fits the context (i.e., whether it is in character) and not by reference to some external criterion.

dramatis personae
the characters in a narrative (or a list thereof). For example, the dramatis personae of Courbet's The Artist's Studio would be Baudelaire, Buchon, Champfleury, Courbet himself, Napoléon III, Proudhon and so on.

drame bourgeois
a slightly more recherché version of bourgeois drama.

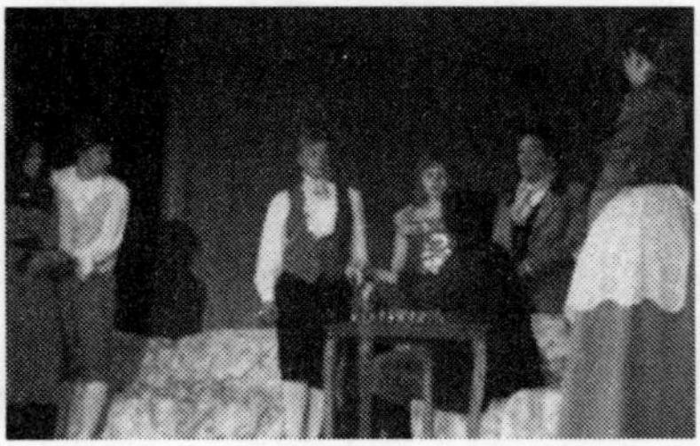

dream-work
the processes by which unconscious desire (i.e., repressed wishes) is 'translated' into acceptable content in a dream. Freud distinguished three such mechanisms: condensation, displacement and secondary elaboration. Dream-work is central to psychological criticism and the first two have been developed further as the psychic mechanisms, making conscious, creative metaphor and metonymy possible.

dualism
1. the Platonic doctrine that the universe is composed of two basic substances, mind and matter.
2. the subsequent philosophical and psychological positions that mind and body are separate entities and/or processes.

duality of structure
synonymous with double articulation.

dumb show
pantomime, originally in the context of a play, but extendable to many early Christian and medieval representations in which religious narratives are acted out, as it were, by figures in conventionalised poses and exaggerated, stereotypical facial expressions.

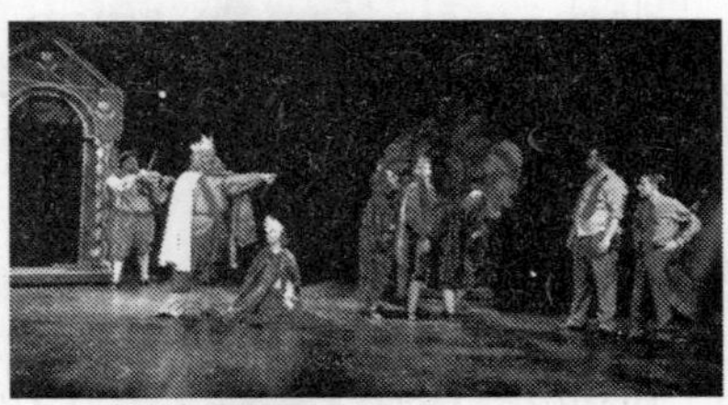

duologue
a play with only two speakers.

DWM
Dead White Male. This is a derogatory reference to the study of the humanities as a

Eurocentric canon made up only of the privileged and the powerful. People oppose this by calling for the inclusion of women, non-whites and the dispossessed.

■ **dynamic character**

a character who changes within a narrative.

■ **dynamic equilibrium**

Piet Mondrian's term to characterise the universal balance achieved by forces in motion. The idea is rather like the yin-yang of Eastern thought, in which all imaginable things can be reduced to paired relations, like light/dark, male/female, good/evil, all of which exist by virtue of their opposite.

■ **dysfunctional**

impaired or abnormal functioning. One hears often of dysfunctional families, for example.

■ **dysphemism**

the opposite of euphemism, conveying a message in a manner that is disproportionately negative. E.g., 'piss off' frequently replaces 'go away'. Images that place great emphasis on negative aspects might be so described, as in Otto Dix's The Trench.

■ **dystopia**

the opposite of utopia. An extremely disagreeable place (construed as an era, a political state or even a state of mind).

■ **eclecticism**

the composition of something by selecting details and stylistic features from a wide variety of sources. Nineteenth-century architecture, for example, was eclectic in its rather derivative adherence to the manners of bygone eras, as in Classical Revival, Gothic Revival and the like. Postmodern architecture is more ironically eclectic, as in Charles Moore's Piazza d'Italia in New Orleans.

■ **economy**

the organisation, structure or mode of operation of a group. More specifically, the system of exchange within an identifiable group, whether the exchange be of money (economy in the widest sense) or of some more ephemeral thing, like meaning.

■ (l')écriture
'Writing', but with connotations taken over from the death of the author to the effect that what is written is an open-ended text, with multiple possibilities of meaning beyond those intended by the author. Some writers use the word 'scription' to indicate much the same idea.

■ effect
something that invariably follows a cause, the consequence of inflection and/or the overall emotional or dramatic impact or tone of an artwork.

■ effect of the real
in art and literature, the creation of a fictive world that appears to be seen through a transparent window, rather than as the result of a particular individual's creative behaviour or the processes of an audience's enunciation.

■ ego
generally, one's conception of the self. More specifically, in psychoanalytical thought, one of three main divisions of the psyche. The ego makes distinctions between the self and the not-self (i.e., the environment) and in the process mediates between the primitive, infantile mind and the moral mind.

■ egocentric
considering the ego as central, as in simple selfishness or in developed philosophies or ethics, which give priority to self-interest.

■ eidetic imagery
mental images with extraordinary vividness, as if actually perceptible.

■ eidos
term for the Platonic conception of the essential.

■ ekphrasis
synonym for description.

■ elaboration
a tactic in rhetoric by which a theme is progressively argued by gradual repetition

with emendations, alterations and the like. Visual equivalents are easy enough to imagine.

elegy
a solemn meditation on death and the like, particularly when presented in a gravely formal manner.

elemental
pertaining to the four basic elements (air, earth, fire and water) and, by analogy, anything fundamental, rudimentary or expressive of the basic forces of nature.

elision
omission of a component, usually of a word or a part thereof (as in contractions like can't). In medieval imagery, illuminated texts frequently had elisions signalled by a short line above the contraction.

elite culture
see **high culture**.

ellipsis
the omission of one or more words whose sense can be easily supplied. For example, in 'Bernini's sculpture reached the zenith of Baroque exuberance, his painting the nadir', the identity of the missing word in the second clause is signalled by 'reached' in the first.

emblem
a picture associated with a motto, usually moralising in tone. An example is a popular print showing King Midas, unable to eat because his touch turns everything to gold, accompanied by the words 'both rich and poor'

embourgeoisement
the suppression of difference in class by attributing to all members of a society the values of the middle class (the bourgeoisie).

emotion
psychological and/or physical reactions to stimuli subjectively experienced as feelings.

emotive
see **mind-set**.

emotivism
also known as emotive theory, emotivism holds that value judgements are neither good nor bad but simply expressions of emotion, like laughing or fear.

empathy
now loosely the same as 'sympathy', i.e., identification with another's feelings, but careful users usually stipulate empathy as an imaginative projection of one's own feelings into an event or object. One should perhaps be suspicious of the latter, inasmuch as it can easily produce meanings that are read into an artwork.

emphasis
any of several means of drawing, special attention to some feature(s) of an artwork for aesthetic impact.

empirical
derived from observation, whether through anecdotes or through controlled experiment.

empower
to enable, to give recognition to, to facilitate self-expression, particularly of marginal groups within a dominant culture.

emulation
thus can mean either 'imitation' or the 'striving to equal or exceed'. As a contemporary technological term, it also means a device allowing a program written for one computer to be run on another computer or a musical instrument which records sounds digitally for playback, manipulation, etc.

enantiomorphs
mirror images, in effect, as a left hand is to a right. As simple as the idea seems to be, it has been used in such difficult Kantian philosophical questions as 'is space relative or absolute'? Students of visual art might care to examine a once-popular conception, similar to some aspects of information theory, that whatever a viewer experiences before an artwork is the exactly

reconstituted emotional expression of the artist.

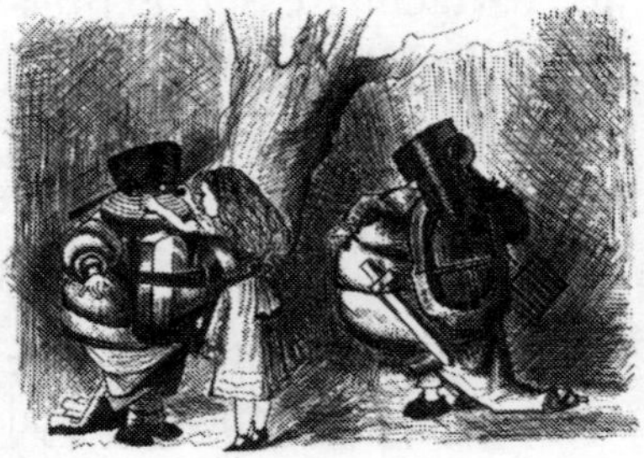

■ encoding

in information theory, the conversion of a message into a form that can be transmitted along a channel. In postmodernist artwriting, the idea is discussed more frequently from the point of view of code and decoding.

■ encomium

in Greek literature, enthusiastic praise, delivered in soberly formal terms, of anyone or anything aside from the gods. Any decidedly glorifying treatment of a subject's visual representation could be described as encomiastic.

■ entelechy

the actuality or truth of a thing, rather than its potentiality. In Aristotelian thought, entelechy was used to distinguish the soul from the body. In vitalist thought, entelechy is an unobservable, hypothetical agent that directs organic processes.

■ enthymeme

a syllogism with a hidden premise. For example, in 'Artists should be seen and not heard. Be quiet, Pablo', the minor premise that Pablo is an artist is suppressed but understood.

■ entropy

originally from the study of thermodynamics, entropy has been used in a variety of ways in other disciplines. In certain sociological circles, for example, the original definition of entropy as the degree to which energy in a system is available to do work becomes a description of how social progress slows and finally stops because social change uses up energy which cannot then be retrieved for reuse in further change. Related is the psychoanalytical usage, in which psychic energy cannot be transferred from the object in which it is originally invested. A more straightforward application of entropy as the tendency of ordered systems to degrade into a state of inanimate uniformity can be seen in the writings of artist Robert Smithson.

■ **epic**
a long narrative, usually in the form of a poem or film, in which the stories of a number of characters are traced against a background of sweeping historical importance, as in Leon Uris's novels. The term is only rarely applied to the visual arts.

■ **epideictic**
now rarely used Aristotelian term for the type of rhetoric used chiefly to please an audience, as in encomium.

■ **epigram**
a concise aphorism with moralising overtones, which ensures that they will have a rich history in visual illustration.

■ **epigraph**
the inscription of a motto or similar on a coin, relief, titlepage and the like. The study of such things collectively is called epigraphy.

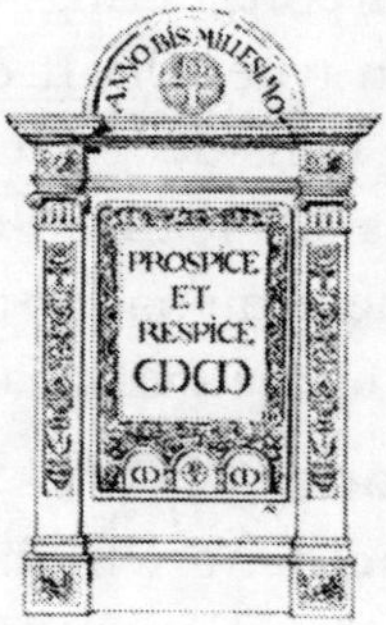

■ **epiphany**
a sudden manifestation of divine insight, as in Bellini's Ecstacy of St. Francis. When the term is used figuratively to indicate a sudden intuitive insight, especially in popular criticism, readers should cautiously note whether the writer is seeking to persuade through emotional rhetoric.

■ **epiphenomenalism**
the doctrine that consciousness is a product of neural activity in the nervous system (i.e., an epiphenomenon of material existence).

■ epiphenomenon

an accessory or accompaniment to some phenomenon, but considered incidental to it and not a causal factor in its development. It might be worth considering whether certain types of art criticism really consider specific artworks basically ignorable epiphenomena of the systems under examination.

■ episode

an incident which, when taken as a step in a sequential series of incidents, regardless of the order of the sequence, constitutes a narrative. The individual scenes in the iconographic programs of medieval churches could be so described.

■ episodic

a literary term applied to structures of stringed episodes, which do not necessarily follow a logical pattern or even seem to develop the plot.

■ epitaph

inscriptions and the like marking a burial place.

■ epithet

a characterising word or phrase appearing with or in place of a name or thing, as in Homer's 'rosy- fingered dawn'. They need not be disparaging, although they often are in satire.

■ epitome

a summary or typical example of something. Chartres Cathedral might be called the epitome of Gothic church design, which would mean not that it represents the best of what was available, but that it is typical of what was available.

■ eponym

a name so closely linked to a characteristic, a place or some other general thing that it comes to stand for that. The principle operates when artists' names are used to characterise general tendencies in the arts.

■ eristic

fond of wrangling, as in people who argue for the sake of argument. The word is sometimes used in place of polemics.

essential copy

Norman Bryson maintains that artwriters who look only for realism in a painting overlook historical and social dimensions in favour of the essential copy, i.e. the empty verisimilitude of the painting's ability to convince the viewer that it 'is' the thing, instead of 'meaning' the thing.

essentialism

any of a variety of notions concerning the primacy of essences, i.e. permanent, unchanging, 'real' identities that lie 'behind' appearances, rather than the temporary, changing, specific manifestations themselves. The most common essentialisms are the Platonic doctrine of universal types and the originally Aristotelian doctrine that things in a particular category all have at least one common characteristic, without which they could not be members of that category.

ethics

popularly, the (moral) standards which a particular group sets to distinguish acceptable behaviour from unacceptable behaviour. Philosophical ethics have a long and complicated history.

ethnic

deriving originally from 'ethnos' (nation or people), ethnic once meant any social group bound by race, customs, language, values, etc. Its current use to indicate any visible minority in a Eurocentric culture is often a thinly veiled reflection of an older use meaning 'heathen'.

ethnocentrism

the tendency to see one's own ethnic group as the norm and all others as marginal.

ethnicity

ethnic identity or the discourse which concerns it.

ethnography

generally, social or cultural anthropology. Among studies of art, the most overtly ethnographic are those, which deal with general patterns in non-Western cultures, rather than with artist and object-centred interpretations, so that individuality and uniqueness are less highly prized than epitome.

■ **ethnology**

sometimes synonymous with ethnography, ethnology is also sometimes distinguished from it by being less focussed on the data gathering of fieldwork and participant observation and more concerned with the historiography of cultures.

■ **ethology**

originally a branch of zoology, ethology counters behaviourism by arguing that certain types of human behaviour are innate genetic developments that had survival value in evolutionary terms. Some of these ideas are creeping into aesthetics in the form of a supposedly universal 'behaviour of art', a kind of investment of value and meaning in what is otherwise valueless and meaningless by means of play and ritual.

■ **ethos**

the distinguishing characteristic, usually of a social group, particularly when it is a case of moral values or beliefs.

■ **etymology**

the study of the origins of words.

■ **euphemism**

the opposite of dysphemism. An expression of an disagreeable state of affairs in mild or oblique terms calculated to avoid unpleasantness or offence. E.g., 'to pass on' is frequently used instead of 'to die'.

■ **ex-centric**

those who have been pushed from a central position or marginalised by a dominant ethnic group, institutional practice or ideology. The artwork of Black American women like Betye Saar and Faith Ringgold and that of North American Native artists like Jane Ash Poitras and James A. Luna is thus said to be ex-centric because it is produced by voices that have been traditionally suppressed. It is accordingly not to be confused with 'eccentric', which means 'deviated from accepted conduct'.

■ excess

in psychological and neurological circles, an excess is the opposite of a deficit. While a cognitive deficit is an impairment of mental function preventing the patient from forming a complete representation of experience in consciousness and thus deriving meaning from it, a cognitive excess is a superabundance of meaning that originates with the patient, not in the outside world.

■ exegesis

interpretation understood chiefly as explanation, originally of the Bible, but now of any text.

■ exemplum virtutis

term used in Robert Rosenblum's Transformations in Late Eighteenth Century Art to describe artworks whose themes are moral lessons or examples of virtue which should be emulated. The theme is particularly common in neoclassicism.

■ exergue

a small space for an inscription, originally on coins and medallions, but now also on any other object, visual or verbal.

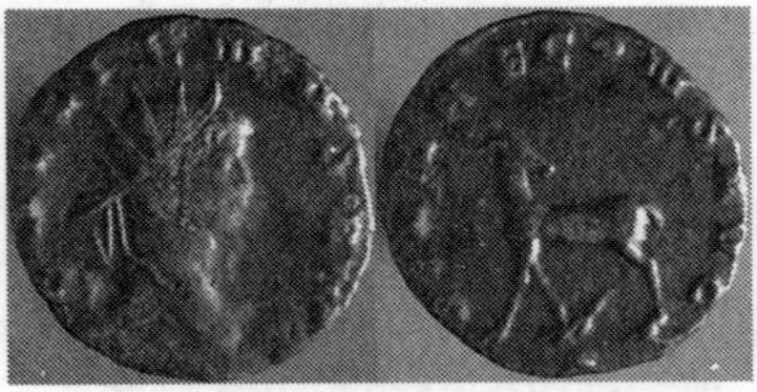

■ expert

one who is supposed to have special authority, experience, knowledge, skills and the like.

■ existential criticism

criticism which downplays or undermines traditional themes and conventional methods, especially those purporting to use scientific disinterestedness, in order to investigate more personal, existential issues, as outlined under existentialism. Probably the most famous proponent is Jean- Paul Sartre.

■ expression theory

probably the most popular and long-standing notion of art is that it is the expression of the artist's emotion. Although such a simple expression theory stretches back as far as Plato, the first person to make the idea a criterion of systematic aesthetic inquiry was Eugène Véron, who wrote in L'Esthétique (1878) that "art is the manifestation of emotion...by expressive arrangements of line, form or colour...[and/or] by a series of gestures, sounds or words governed by a particular rhythmical cadence." While Leo Tolstoy, Benedeto Croce and many others have made significant contributions, the most thorough development of expression theory is generally agreed to be that of R. G. Collingwood. Collingwood distinguished very carefully between art and craft on the grounds that true art involved the genuine expression of an emotion and its recreation in the spectator. He also argued that true expression was not a simple matter of having an emotion and showing it because expression meant a coming to self-awareness.

■ expressionism

any of various styles and/or movements in art, giving priority to the expression of inner experience, particularly where the manifestation is conspicuously deformed or paralinguistically altered.

■ expressive

vague, overused adjective indicating vivid or especially apt descriptions, depictions, performances and the like, of personal moods or sentiments.

■ expressive theory

more or less a synonym for expression theory, used in the literary criticism of M. H. Abrams.

extensional definitions

definitions which identify members of the class of things named by that term (for example, visual arts means painting, photography, printmaking, sculpture, etc.). Such definitions link our experience to the world. Without them, all words would be circular.

extralinguistic

Paul Ricoeur uses this word to refer to the expressivity of being: "while linguistics moves inside the enclosure of a self-sufficient universe and encounters only intrasignificant relations..., hermeneutics is ruled by the open state of the universe of signs." The term is thus not to be confused with paralinguistic.

extrinsic

external, extraneous, not forming part of or belonging to a thing. In some artwriting, contextual information is characterised as extrinsic.

fable

any brief tale or fictitious narrative, especially when peopled by talking animals or objects and aimed at teaching a moral lesson.

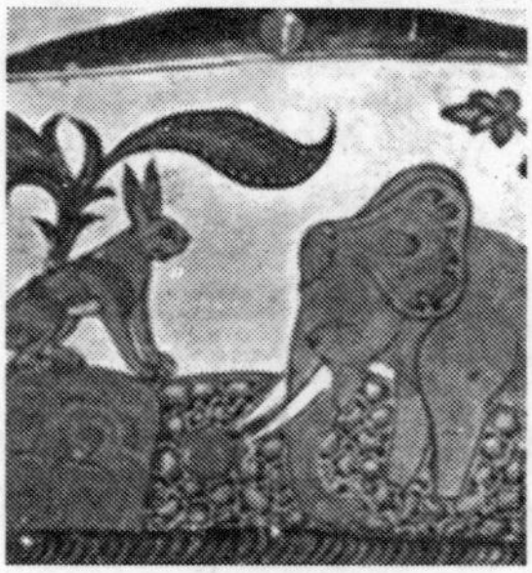

fabula

latin for conversation, play or story. Some writers substitute fabula for plot.

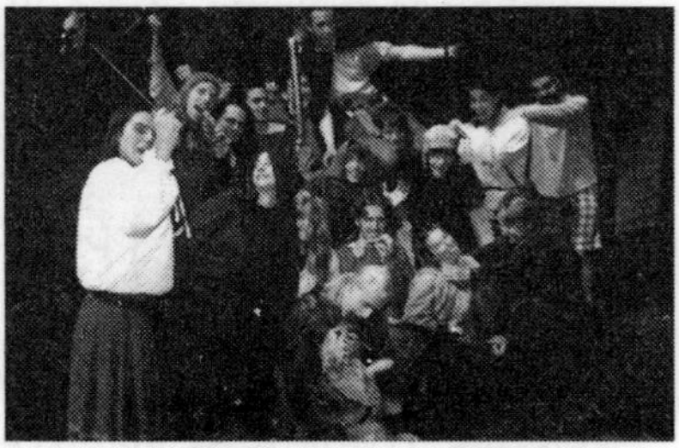

fallacies

most specifically, any of various types of argument in which invalid reasoning is used. More loosely, however, the word is used to indicate any error (real or imagined) or wrong-headed belief, as in affective fallacy, biographical fallacy, genetic fallacy, intentional fallacy, pathetic fallacy, stratigraphic fallacy.

■ **false consciousness**

a much used term originating with Marx, indicating the failure of the typical human mind to develop any sophisticated awareness of its rooting in historically specific circumstances. Instead of being conscious of how its abilities, contents, habits and patterns are shaped by circumstances, such a consciousness is not really a material consciousness at all but only conceives of itself as such.

■ **falsification**

according to Karl Popper, a more useful process than verification in distinguishing science from non-science. Universal claims like 'all swans are white' cannot be verified because one can never collect all swans to prove to it. However, one can falsify the statement simply by producing one black swan. Science thus can never reach a point at which it can claim, without risk of error, that it has reached the final truth.

■ **fancy**

at one time a synonym of 'imagination', fancy was distinguished from it and made subordinate in late eighteenth-century academic thought. As a result, where imagination means the power to create something unprecedented, fancy has come to mean a certain resourcefulness in manipulating the already given.

■ **fantastic**

there is no unequivocal consensus, but 'fantastic' is sometimes used to indicate an imaginative, subjective world of inner expression that transcends mere fantasy or science fiction.

■ **fantasy**

any conscious break with reality, whether in the relatively benign forms of caprices and daydreams or in the more psychologically charged delusions and hallucinations.

■ farce

a narrative depending on improbable situations, outlandish characters, grotesque language and imagery, rather than on well-wrought plot and the like. The term usually carries a spin of 'low comedy'. When presented in the form 'farce-comedy', the term implies high comedy that occasionally makes use of farce elements, as in Woody Allen's later films.

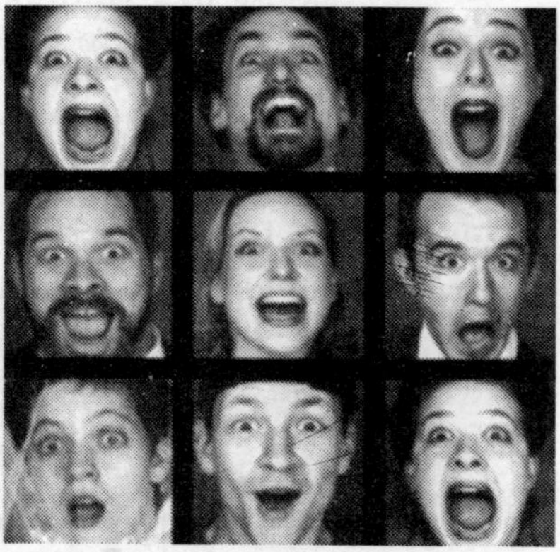

■ farce-comedy

see **farce**.

■ fascist feminism

a brand of feminism which is thought by its opponents to be symptomatic of right-wing politics, central dictatorial control or simply a profound lack of critical self-consciousness.

■ faux amis

false cognates, as in the French 'assister à' (to attend) versus the English 'assist' (to give aid).

■ femicide

title of a 1992 book by Jill Radford describing the misogynous killing of women by men.

■ femi-nazi

derogatory term for fascist feminism, popularised by abrasive radio personality Rush Limbaugh.

■ feminism

although some dictionaries define 'feminism' simply as the advocacy of the rights and equality of women in economic, political and social contexts, there are actually all sorts of feminisms and feminist practices. Moreover, some feminists disagree profoundly with others. Where Heidi Göttner-Abendroth calls for a matriarchal aesthetic that transcends historical specifics, for example, Linda Nochlin once wrote that such a feminism was essentialist and the antithesis of historical action. The two basic types of feminist interpretation are what Elaine Showalter called feminist criticism and gynocriticism (works about women versus works by women).

■ feminist criticism

Showalter's term for criticism of the artistic productions of male authors, especially (but not necessarily) in their treatment of the image of women and in their relations to a female audience.

■ field

a physical plane, a sphere of activity, a context, a discourse, the totality of an individual's perceptions in a given period or the psychological representation in consciousness of the same and so on.

■ field dependent

one who cannot ignore irrelevant data in a perceptual field is said to be field dependent. When one uses the idea in a critique of artwriting, one must be careful to ascertain that the data are genuinely irrelevant to a particular task.

■ field independent

one who can ignore irrelevant data in a perceptual field is said to be field independent. Field theory argues that such a person is behaviourally normal, whereas a field dependent person is not.

■ figuration

an act of representation in figures.

■ figurative

1. any expression of one thing in terms of another thing, by means of language that rejects the literal in favour of a figure of speech or a trope. Strangely, audiences often forget to consider the figurative in visual images, particularly photog-

raphy, even though they readily recognise that common speech is riddled with figurative expressions like 'she was on cloud nine'. Visual images are no less figurative, ranging from pure conventions like personifications to more imaginative tropes.

2. artwriters sometimes use 'figurative' simply to mean that an image contains recognisable images. Since this usage does not distinguish between literal and figurative in the sense given above, it is considerably less precise.

■ figure

a numerical or other symbol, a written or printed character, a graphic representation of a form, a figure of speech, etc.

■ figure poem

another name for carmen figuratum.

■ figure of sight

see **figure of speech**.

■ figure of speech

any use of language that replaces a literal expression (e.g., 'he was angry') with an indirect one, like the conventional statement 'he was beside himself'. Tropes are generally more inventive and individual figures of speech. (They were once called 'figures of thought' to distinguish them from more conventional expressions, but that usage is outdated.) Some literary critics have argued that there are 'figures of sound', meaning such things as alliteration, poetic repetition and rhythm. A hypothetical 'figure of sight' could go either way, being either a matter of formal repetition or figurative language in visual imagery.

■ figure of thought

see **figure of speech**.

■ filiopietistic

pertaining to an excessive reverence of ancestors or tradition. Some coffee-table type books which praise artists unreservedly as geniuses could be described as filiopietistic.

■ fine art

visual art considered primarily for its aesthetic or theoretical character, including its meaning and significance independent of practical application, as opposed to commercial art.

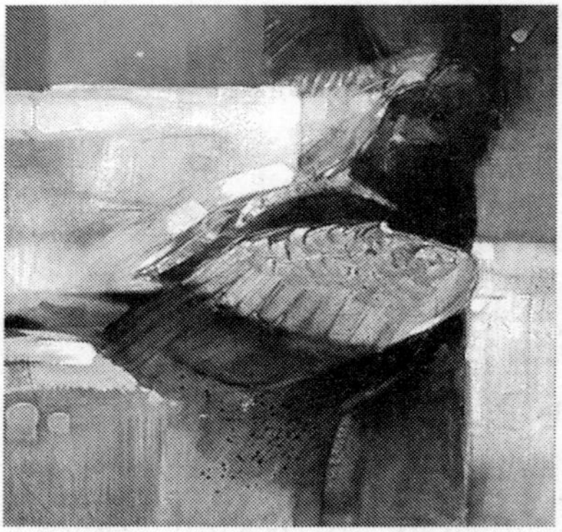

■ fixation pause

brief moments between saccades during which the eyeball is not moving and something comes into focus. The meaning of a printed word is conveyed during such a moment, giving some idea of the rapidity with which meaning is constructed by a succession of perceptual instants.

■ flat

although it is an oversimplification of Clement Greenberg's position, artists and artwriters of the 1960s and early 1970s agreed with his assertion that the essential characteristic of painting was its flatness. This led to post-painterly abstraction on the one hand and to minimalism on the other.

■ flavour

a predominant quality or characteristic, as in the exotic flavour of a Delacroix painting.

■ foil

originally, a slip of shiny metal placed under a translucent jewel to increase the amount of light it reflects. By extension, the term is commonly used in literary criticism to refer to characters whose personalities contrast those of the protagonist in order to show the latter in a better light.

■ folk art

traditional representations, usually bound by conventions in both form and content, of a folkloric character and usually made by persons without institutionalised training.

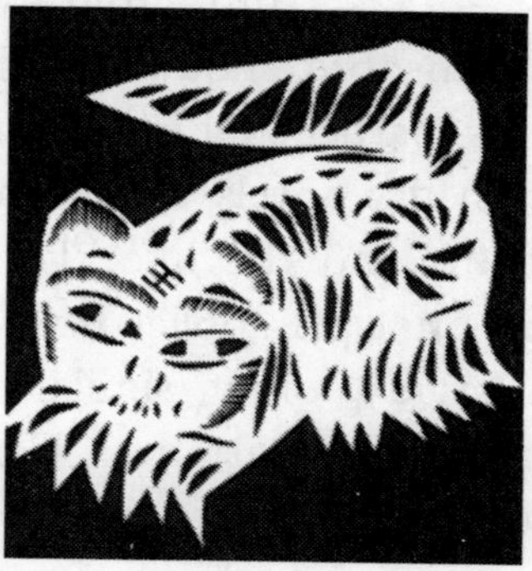

■ folk etymology

where etymology, deriving from the Greek etymon (true), is the study of the literal meanings of words according to their origins, folk etymology is the unsystematic application of similar principles, sometimes leading to errors, faux amis and fanciful connections where there are none.

■ folklore

traditional customs, fables, legends, myths, proverbs, sayings, tales and the like. Folklore has had a direct influence on literature and art.

■ foreground

1. the part of a field of vision that is closest to the audience.

2. to give priority to one aspect of a thing over another.

■ forensic

Aristotelian term for that type of rhetoric used chiefly to condemn the actions of others.

■ forgery

the direct imitation of another artist's manner for the purpose of defrauding an audience. Because fraud is involved, forgery is not to be confused with appropriation.

■ form

the constituent elements of a work of art, independent of their meaning. Formal elements are primary features which are not a matter of semantic significance, including colour, dimensions, line, mass, medium, scale, shape, space, texture, value and their corollaries and secondary features which are the relations of the primary features with one another, including balance, contrast, dominance, harmony, movement, proportion, proximity, rhythm, similarity, unity and variety.

■ **formal**
pertaining to the form of a work. Not to be confused with 'ceremonial' or 'stately', since formal elements can be quite informal in character.

■ **formal analysis**
the study of a work of art with reference to its form, rather than to its content or context.

■ **formalism**
any of several types of art making or criticism which foreground form. Because generic formalism was once institutionally entrenched as the most powerful critical approach, artists frequently produced works, which catered specifically to it, rather than to self-expression (foregrounding content) or social responsibility (foregrounding context).

■ **formal language**
any uninterpreted system of signs, as in formal logic.

■ **formula**
a cliché in narrative form. Any immediately recognisable sequence of events, particularly common in romance novels, television sitcoms and the like. The same principle applies in visual art exploiting similarly unchallenging narratives, like Paul Delaroche's Tudor history paintings.

■ **formulaic**
an adjective describing anything prepared to formula.

■ **Foucauldian**
pertaining to the ideas of Michel Foucault.

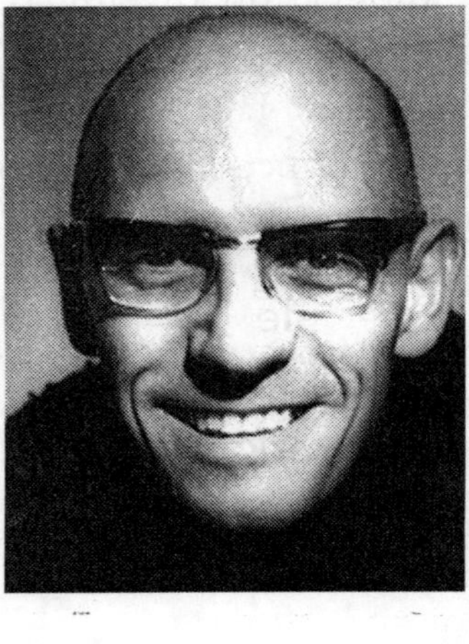

■ fragmentation
postmodern discourse, because it lacks uniformity, is often said to be fragmented, i.e. broken, discontinuous, incomplete, open-ended, etc. Fragmentation is thus desirable because it avoids closure.

■ frame
although a frame can be anything composed of parts fitting together (like the physical frame of an athlete or a building), the term most often indicates an enclosing border or boundary, both literally and figuratively. In literary studies, it is common to find the idea applied in the frame-tale or framework story, both of which refer to a story told within another story, as in Shelley's Frankenstein, which is told via the letters of a northern explorer.

■ frame-tale
see **frame**.

■ framework story
see **frame**.

■ framing
see **frame**.

■ functions of art
introductory books and study guides on art history usually give a variation of the following as the basic functions of art: to adorn, to beautify, to express, to illustrate, to mediate, to persuade, to record, to redefine reality and to redefine art.

■ fundamental image
a predominant image, aspect or unifying characteristic of a text, apart from a distinct and repeated metaphor or other trope, which would be called a controlling image.

■ fusion of horizons
Gadamer's term in Truth and Method for the fundamental differences (and/or the reconciliation of same) between the perspectives of author and audience. Of horizon of expectations.

■ Gadamerian
pertaining to the ideas of Hans-Georg Gadamer.

Ganz andere, das

the 'wholly other', which Georges Bataille developed into his theory of heterology. The phrase occurs in the religious writings of Soren Kierkegaard and Karl Barth, but it is most intimately associated with the theologian Rudolph Otto, whose The Idea of the Holy describes it is as the inexplicable otherness of God.

gaze

see **gaze and glance**.

gaze and glance

Norman Bryson's Vision and Painting critiques realism in painting because its apparent invisibility as technique and as meaning in a social formation appeals to an ahistorical, disembodied, programmatic 'gaze'. In contrast, he describes the 'glance' as anchored in history, in body, in desire and in improvisation. The latter is preferable because it allows for an aesthetic of disruption. The terminology has become quite fashionable and can be found nearly anywhere.

geistesgeschichte

the history of ideas or intellectual history. Wilhelm Dilthey argued that if the natural sciences explain events as the results of causal laws, cultural science should explain events in terms of the meanings and intentions that people give them. These meanings and intentions, however are informed by historical and social change, particularly the total global outlook peculiar to a given period. Geistesgeschichte made inroads into art history in Max Dvoràk's Idealism and Naturalism in Gothic Art.

gender

J. P. Chaplin's Dictionary of Psychology lists 'gender' simply as 'sex — male or female', while 'gender identity' is given as 'one's sense of being male or female'. In contemporary artwriting, 'gender' usually means the latter of these two.

■ gender identity
see **gender**.

■ gender symmetry
the presumption that for each characteristic of one gender there is some complementary opposite in the other gender. This line of reasoning is now disparaged because it lends itself easily to essentialism. E.g., if men are strong, women are weak. If men are competitors, women are collaborators.

■ genderlect
gender-based differences in conversational style. The two basic genderlects are rapport-talk and report-talk. One wonders if the idea might be used to revise essentialist definitions of gender-based aesthetic sensibilities, as in matriarchal aesthetic.

■ general economy
a term of Bataillean origin, but most recently used by Steve McCaffery in North of Intention to indicate 'the distribution and circulation of the numerous forces and intensities that saturate a text'. It is thus basically a synonym for the interrelations of content and context.

■ generalisation
a common structure in informal logic: some members of a group have characteristic X, therefore, members of the group in general have characteristic X. Obviously, a valid generalisation must be based on a representative sample that is of reasonable size and is free of bias.

■ genetic fallacy
the presumption that because a certain condition obtains today, it must always have been such and vice versa. E.g., that people evolved from some kind of apes indicates that people are now higher apes.

■ Geneva school
influential literary school of thought which asserted that a text is the existential expression of an individual consciousness. Accordingly, Geneva school criticism is relatively uninterested in the

text as a physical object and more interested in its affective properties.

■ genius

one of the more overworked conceptions in traditional artwriting, 'genius' originally referred to an attendant spirit or tutelary deity of the sort seen sprinkling holy water in Assyrian reliefs. It has become synonymous with transcendent intellectual or creative power and as such is a cliché in basically Romantic descriptions of divinely inspired artists outside history. In postmodernism, nothing is seen as outside history and all conceptions of genius are discarded or at least made secondary to such things as the social formation.

■ genre

see **genres**.

■ genre criticism

criticism which foregrounds genres.

■ genres

1. the various categories of subject matter in the traditional academic hierarchy, in descending order of importance: history, megalography, mythology, religion, portraiture, genre, landscape, still-life and rhopography.
2. a little confusingly, one of the genres is 'genre', the depiction of everyday life, ordinary folk and common activities.

■ genus

see **definitional rules**.

■ gesamtkunstwerk

German expression for complete or total artwork, usually associated with Richard Wagner's theatrical integrations of drama, music and spectacle. The idea is applied by analogy to any grandiose work in which a variety of arts contribute to a shared goal, as in the blended architecture, painting and sculpture of Gianlorenzo Bernini's Ecstacy of St. Teresa in the Cornaro Chapel.

■ gestalt

German word meaning 'configuration', 'figure' or any

whole pattern with characteristics different from its parts. E.g., the tune of a song is such a pattern because it does not appear in the individual notes.

■ gestalt factors
conditions which create the perceived effect of a unitary figure (closure) rather than a relation of parts. The most frequently mentioned are contiguity, contrast, proximity and similarity. For example, eight vertical lines will read as four bars if they are arranged in pairs rather than evenly spaced. Such effects are routinely discussed in artwriting involving the psychology of perception and are, as a result, mostly a matter of visual patterns.

■ gestalt psychology
the study of human behaviour and experience as a whole phenomenon. Consciousness, for example, cannot be studied analytically because the analysis would break it into parts which would cease to bear any resemblance to it.

■ gift
a sociological term relating to exchange rituals (e.g., potlatches) and the like in tribal culture.

■ glance
see **gaze and glance**.

■ global
general, comprehensive, embracing all factors within the field at hand.

■ golden section
a mythical proportion which was once fashionable in discussions of compositions with pretensions to perfect harmony and eternal gracefulness. Unfortunately, it can be found just about anywhere one chooses to look for it. It is usually expressed as '(a:b as b:[a+b])' or the subdivision of a line or any other figure, area, etc., such that the smaller part is to the larger part as the larger part is to the whole.

■ gouache
see **body colour**.

■ **gram**

see **grammatology**.

■ **grammatology**

grammatology originally meant only the study of writing as the systematic presentation of meaning in graphic codes and representations. Since Jacques Derrida's Of Grammatology, grammatology has taken on a far more philosophical tone. Traditional discussions of language maintain that speech existed prior to writing. Derrida argues the opposite. While the smallest meaningful unit of speech would be the morpheme, the smallest unit of writing is the 'gram', the mark or trace. The individual grams of a writing have no essential meaning resulting from an actual bond with the things they describe or indicate. Meaning simply arises from the differences between grams and the deferral of meaning that a reader must undertake in order to prevent false closure.

■ **grand récit**

French term for metanarrative.

■ **ground**

a basis for action, argument or belief.

■ **groundlessness**

Derrida's Truth in Painting uses the metaphor of an upturned boot in a painting by Van Gogh to confirm the groundlessness of logocentric assertions of essential meaning.

■ **guilt by association**

a tactic in informal logic: artist X knows artist Y well. Artist Y is suspicious, therefore, artist X is suspicious. The tactic works in a valid argument only when the alleged association genuinely exists, when Y is demonstrably suspicious (or whatever) and when there are no relevant premises (such as unstated causal arguments) to differentiate X from Y. The tactic is rarely identified as such in art history, but it is very common, as when Neoplatonists are linked to Michelangelo or linguistic theorists are to postmodern artists.

■ gynocentric
anything which foregrounds a putatively essential feminine principle can be considered gynocentric.

■ gynocriticism
Elaine Showalter's term for the criticism and interpretation of works by women authors.

■ gynophobia
irrational fear of women.

■ habitus
a synonym for social formation.

■ hagiography
writing about saints. Traditionally, saints are not recognised as such until they have been officially canonised. By extension then, any type of artwriting giving undue praise to an artist or attempting principally to identify an important contribution to an art-historical canon is implicitly a hagiography. In official religious hagiography, certain criteria must be met. The most well-known of these are miracles and martyrdom. The straightforward analogies for these in art history are masterpieces and bohemianism.

■ hamartia
frequently translated as 'tragic flaw', hamartia is simply a mishap or human frailty, which leads to someone's reversal of fortune.

■ hearsay
a legal term denoting evidence not based on a witness personal knowledge, but on information reported to him by someone else.

■ hebraism
the subordination of everything to principles of obedient conduct. Matthew Arnold uses the term in Culture and Anarchy to signify 'strictness of conscience', in contrast to Hellenism's 'spontaneity of conscience'. The contrast is thus between duty and curiosity.

hedonism
although it roots are genuinely philosophical, hedonism is now taken to mean sensual gratification as an end in itself. The term pops up in discussions of the work of Henri Matisse, Claude Monet and other artists who seem to have made a point of avoiding troubling subject matter or politically specific themes.

hegemony
often linked to the writings of Antonio Gramsci, but by no means exclusive to them, 'hegemony' means predominant influence, especially when it involves coercion, as in colonialism. One reads frequently of the cultural hegemony of the capital over the provinces, the economic hegemony of the middle class over the working class, etc.

Heideggerian
pertaining to the ideas of Martin Heidegger.

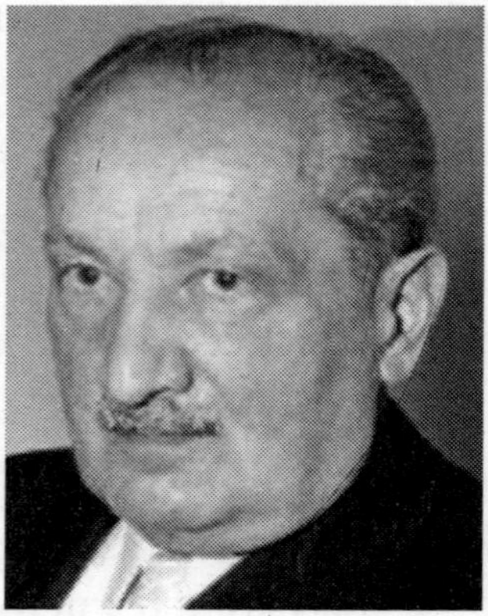

heliography
see **photography**.

hellenism
the subordination of everything to the intellect, even sensual beauty.

heresy of paraphrase
the notion that anything — an artwork, text, utterance, etc. — means what it means only in its original form, so that any abbreviation, paraphrase, translation or other form of representation introduces distortions, simplifications and misunderstandings.

herstory
a neologism invented because of the false perception of affinity between 'history'

and 'his story'. Despite the etymological fallacy, 'herstory' is an economical way to describe women's history and the feminist project of dismantling a male-only canon.

■ heterodoxy
ideas not in accordance with or critical of established doctrine or received opinion.

■ heterogeneity
the state of being fundamentally different in kind.

■ heteroglossia
'Different tongues' or 'the speech of others'. Mikhail Bakhtin coined the word to describe multiple voices in a text.

■ heterological statements
a statement which is not true of itself. For example, 'Italian', which is not an Italian word.

■ heuristic
stimulating interest in order to make new discoveries and formulations, and/or a teaching method to encourage students to discover for themselves. The term is fairly common in current artwriting.

■ hierarchical
the defining characteristic of any system of persons of things given different ranks or statuses, as in a governmental hierarchy.

■ hieratic
originally, 'sacred' or 'priestly'. The term is routinely used to designate a formal, conventional and conceptual style like that in the art of ancient Egypt or the Byzantine Empire. Potential antonyms are demotic and perceptual.

■ hieronymy
originally, 'sacred naming'. The term now means the granting of special status to something by virtue of the way it is named.

■ high art (culture)
until recently, there was a distinction between high art and low art. Where the former supposedly consisted of the

meticulous expression in fine materials of refined or noble sentiment, the latter was the shoddy manufacturing in inferior materials of superficial kitsch. Moreover, the assumption always was that appreciation of the former depended on such things as intelligence, social standing, educated taste and a willingness to be challenged. In contrast, the latter simply catered to popular taste, unreflective acceptance of realism and a certain 'couch potato' mentality. Although many earlier artists took inspiration from popular and folk art, the most systematic approaches towards blurring the differences between high and low art were taken by Cubism, Dada and Surrealism. We now find that formerly 'high' artists are approaching mainstream celebrity status.

■ highlight

the point at which an object reflects the greatest light or the representation of same in drawing, painting, photography, watercolour, etc. Works which follow the logic of perception tend to orient highlights in such a way that the direction of the light source can be deduced from them, but there is no shortage of examples which ignore this principle and use highlights in a rather more intuitive manner.

■ historical criticism

any criticism which attempts to describe, explain or recreate the meaning that a work had in its original context, rather than what it might mean to later generations.

■ historical materialism

the foundation of Marx's materialist theory of history: that the consciousness of men does not determine the social formation, but that the social formation, particularly the economic structure of society, determines consciousness, independent of the will of men.

■ historical methodolo-

gies

those types of criticism which foreground context, especially information of the environmental or secondary sort.

■ historicism

any of a variety of approaches which give priority to history, specifically with the implications that all of life and reality are historically conditioned and that each historical phenomenon must be interpreted according to its own terms.

■ historicity

the historical actuality of a thing, as opposed to putative timelessness.

■ historiography

the theory and practice of historical writing, especially history about history. In artwriting, this usually takes the form of extended historical commentaries on the writings of key art historians.

■ holism

the philosophical notion that the structure and behaviour of a system or an organism in its entirety cannot be explained solely as the sum of the operations of its parts.

■ homage

reverence or tribute, as a serf might give to his lord or an apostle to his master. Artists throughout history have paid homage in various ways to those who influence them.

■ homeostasis

the tendency to maintain constant functioning of organic processes or to attempt to restore constancy when one of the processes is disturbed.

■ homo duplex

man conceived as having two distinct natures, the body and the mind.

■ homological statements

statements which are true of themselves, as 'English' is an English word.

■ homology

a correspondence, relation or similarity between structures. In sociological writings, the term is likely to refer to a metaphorical match between the values of a group and its lifestyle.

■ **homophobic**
irrational fear and/or persecution of homosexuals.

■ **horizon**
the limit or range of perception, knowledge, etc.

■ **horizon of expectations**
the range of values — aesthetic, economic, moral, religious, social, symbolic, etc. — a given audience anticipates it will encounter in an artwork. The work functions either by meeting those expectations or by challenging them. The idea is central to reception-theory.

■ **horror vacui**
a tendency, sometimes characterised as medieval or primitive, to fill all the available pictorial space with decorative or other motifs, as if 'afraid of a vacuum'.

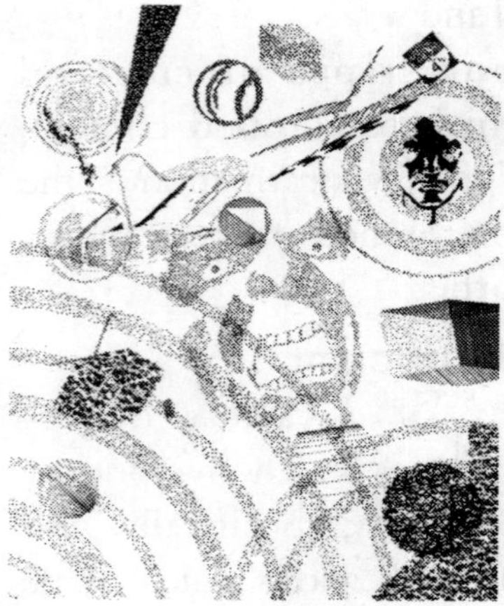

■ **hubris**
arrogance, insolence or pride that leads to misfortune.

■ **hue**
see **colour**.

■ **humanism**
any attitude that gives priority to human endeavours, rather than to those of the gods, the spirits, the animals or any other non-human thing. The term is frequently qualified, as in 'Renaissance humanism', which is characterised by a love of the achievements of the Greco-Roman world, an optimism that humans are inherently endowed with the skills necessary to reshape the world according to their own needs

and a belief in inherent human dignity. While the Renaissance humanists did not see their enlightened self-interest as a contradiction of their Christianity, a few recent demagogues identify 'secular humanism' as a tacitly atheistic preoccupation with human affairs.

■ Husserlian

pertaining to the ideas of Edmund Husserl.

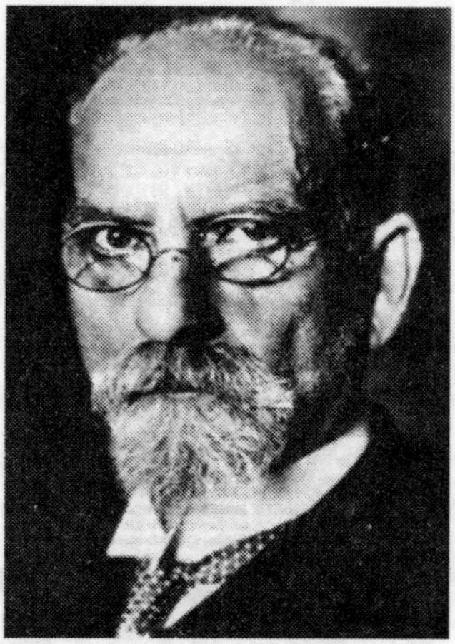

■ hyperbole

exaggeration, whether used simply for effect or because of linguistic inflation. Some Baroque ceiling paintings are extravagantly hyperbolic, as in Pozzo's Allegory of the Missionary Work of the Jesuits on the vault of S. Ignazio, Rome.

■ hyperethnicity

a serious preoccupation with ethnicity. The word should be used with care since some opponents of political correctness use it in a thinly veiled contemptuous manner.

■ hyphenation

a common postmodern technique to draw attention to hidden political and other agendas in supposedly apolitical words. Examples include 'dis-possessed' (Mary Daly, Gyn/Ecology), 'photo-graphed' (Jacques Lacan, 'What is a Picture?' Four Fundamental Concepts of Psycho-Analysis), etc.

■ hypocrisy

pretending to be what one is not or to believe what one does not. The idea should be discussed with reference to traditional myths about artistic bohemianism and genius, as well as to new ones like anti-intellectualism and political correctness.

■ **iatrogenic disease**
disorders caused by treatment for a previous ailment or by the practices of the physician, as in the case of a patient who seeks medical help and develops debilitating side-effects or is abused by the doctor, creating symptoms of mental illness.

■ **icon**
1. a picture, image or representation. In conventional art history, 'icon' generally refers to images of sacred personages in the Byzantine and Greek Orthodox traditions. 2. in various newer approaches, especially those influenced by Peircean semiotics, 'icon' means a signifier which resembles that which it signifies. Of course, this is much more common in visual imagery than in spoken language, although there are examples like onomatopoeia. 3. in popular writing, 'icon' is sometimes taken to mean a celebrity who has come to represent the essence of some quality or characteristic, as Marilyn Monroe was an icon of a certain type of feminine sensuality.

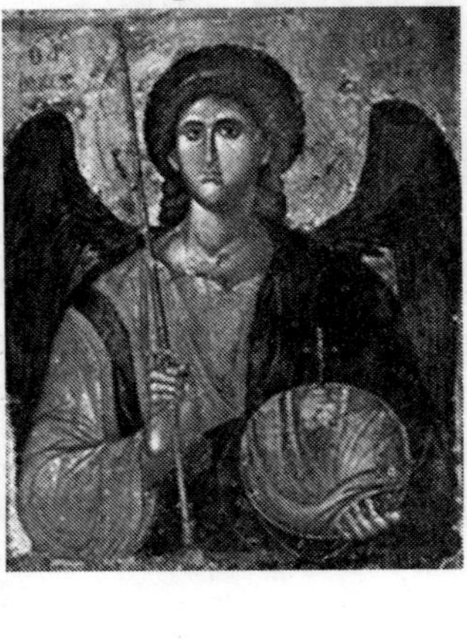

■ **iconicity**
resemblance, the defining characteristic of an icon.

■ **iconoclasm**
1. the destruction of images, especially those receiving religious veneration.
2. by extension, the breaking of traditions, doctrines, convictions, practices, etc.

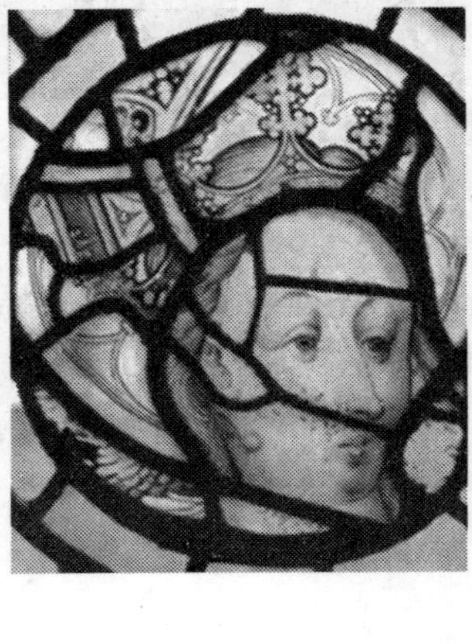

iconography

the study of subject matter and symbolism in the visual arts, especially with reference to verifiable traditions, visual dictionaries and the like.

iconology

the study of iconography with greater emphasis on historical and contextual constraints on the possibilities of meaning. Erwin Panofsky and Aby Warburg are arguably the most famous practitioners.

iconophobic

a rare neologism meaning irrational fear of images. It has recently been used to describe the conservative desire to suppress the more explicitly sexual images of such artists as Robert Mapplethorpe.

id

that portion of the psyche which is the seat of the libido, out of reach of the outside world, driven only to satisfy the basic urges of the body.

idealism

1. in art, the elimination of what is undesirable in the treatment of anything, as in a visual image, until it reaches a predetermined standard of perfection.

2. in philosophy, any of a number of theories sharing the notion the reality has no objective existence but is produced in some way by the mind.

ideological effect

ideology works by making what is economic/political/social and historically contingent appear apolitical and timeless. This process needs to be unconscious, so it functions by creating myths like common sense. The resultant appearance of naturalness (for example, the illusion that sense is genuinely common) is said to be the ideological effect.

ideology

the philosopher Destutt de Tracy coined this word in the early nineteenth century to describe a science of ideas which would reveal unconscious habits of mind like prejudice and class consciousness. Thus it means beliefs, horizons of expectations, ideals, Weltanschauungen and the like as interpretive mechanisms superimposed onto the world by identifiable social groups to impart some sense of order to their experience of it.

■ identity

sameness. The distinguishing character of an individual or social group.

■ idiolect

the speech patterns peculiar to a particular individual, usually in a particular period of his or her life. The farther art is from language — in the sense that it does not subscribe to rules which guarantee intelligible dialogue — then the closer it is to idiolect. This is a profitable analogy since traditional artwriting has usually prized works which are readily identifiable as the productions of specific individuals.

■ idiom

a figurative expression in one language that cannot be translated literally into another, as in 'carrying on' (for 'foolishness') or an expression whose meaning cannot be deduced from the sum of the meanings of its constituent elements, as in 'kick the bucket' (for 'die').

■ idyll

conventionally, a charmingly simple, pastoral and/or sentimental written work. By extension, anything that exhibits similar characteristics, as in Giorgione's Concert champêtre.

■ illiberal education

title of a controversial popular book by Dinesh D'Souza espousing an extremely conservative position in the debate on political correctness. D'Souza's thesis is that postmodern thinkers are literally attacking 'common sense', free speech and traditional scholarship and in so doing are destroying the value and integrity of American education.

illusionism
the principle characteristic of an artwork, which attempts to convince viewers that they are not looking at a representation but at the thing itself. In other words, illusionism means making an image as 'realistic', in the conventional sense of the word, as possible. Especially when accompanied by the word 'optical', 'illusion' is often used to indicate an image which we recognise as playing a deliberate trick on us, like alternating figures. This is precisely not what is meant by 'illusionism', which refers instead to coherent images which pass for the real.

image
in Ways of Seeing, John Berger stipulated that 'image' means a 'sight which has been created or reproduced..., detached from the place and time in which it first made its appearance and preserved'. In other words, an image is an aspect of culture, not nature. Since images are made by humans, they embody 'ways of seeing' — i.e., the assumptions, desires and values of the makers. The implication then, is that an image cannot be an unmediated reality.

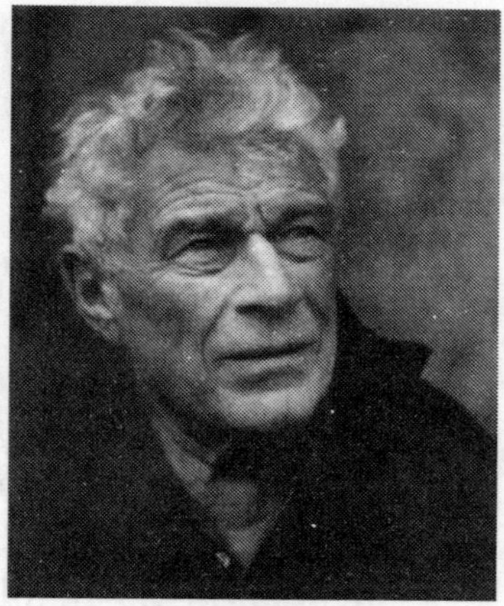

John Berger

imaginary
translation of Lacanian term imaginaire, meaning the psychological dimension of all images, conscious and/or unconscious, whether simply imagined or genuinely perceived. Lacan once felt the imaginary was the most basic psychological process, but he later felt that the

imaginary was displaced by the Symbolic.

imagination
see **fancy**.

imago
an idealised recollection of a cherished person, formed during childhood and very resistant to subsequent change.

imbrication
a successive overlapping, like shingles or tiles. The term has become fashionable as a figurative description of the ways meaning is produced by the interrelations of various forces, rather than in a linear, non-reversible manner.

imitation
a close copy, as in all art which endeavours to reproduce natural appearances. Imitation has played a role in aesthetics since Plato, who banished artists from his hypothetical republic. Material things, he argued, are imperfect reflections of the ideal forms underlying all existence. As an imperfect reflection of something already imperfect, art could only lead men further from the truth.

imperialism
the expansion of a state's authority through the procurement of territory, typically through conquest and the suppression and exploitation of the native populace. Although historical applications involved conscious policies of dominant states, current references often target unconscious attitudes, as in Eurocentrism. As such, imperialism is a central issue in debates on political correctness.

implied artist
see **implied author**.

implied author
Wayne Booth's The Rhetoric of Fiction distinguishes between the real author of a literary work and the author implied by the fiction in the work. The conception is close to Aristotle's ethos. Note, however, that an im-

plied author can actually have the same name as the real author. There is material for a reconsideration of the role of the visual artist along analogous lines.

■ implied reader

in The Implied Reader and The Act of Reading, Wolfgang Iser maintains that one of the functions of a text is to construct a conception of a hypothetical reader who will possess all the propensities required for the text to create the effect of meaning. The implied reader, therefore, exists within the text and not in external reality. A similar phenomenon occurs in some visual art which achieves a meaning effect with an implied viewer, as in Velázquez' Las Meninas, Manet's Bar at the Folies-Bergère and numerous other examples.

■ implied viewer

see **implied reader**.

■ impoverishment

reduction to poverty. Depletion of something considered valuable.

■ imprecation

a curse. There are historical precedents for visual images having the power to curse the viewer, simply by having been looked at. Notorious examples are the curse of the mummy's tomb and the sight of Medusa turning men to stone. This term is not to be confused with imbrication.

■ imprimatur

literally, 'let it be printed', a term originally signifying an ecclesiastical stamp of approval to publish something. By extension, the endorsement of critics who exercise, according to their enemies, too much influence on public taste.

■ improvisation

a work which places emphasis on spontaneous performance without premeditation or at least without the appearance of premeditation. Improvisation can be found in varying degrees in virtually all art forms, from film to literature, dance to painting. In many of these, the improvisation is something which is suggested by, but departs from, specific features of a text, as in a written piece of music which is spun into something quite different by a performer.

■ inauthentic

in existentialism, the unreflective submission of self to circumstances, allowing an exterior, alien world to buffet oneself about without exercising any choice.

■ incantation

a spell, formula or ritualistic chant purporting to have magical power, as in the famous witches' chants in Macbeth. The device is occasionally used quite consciously in visual art.

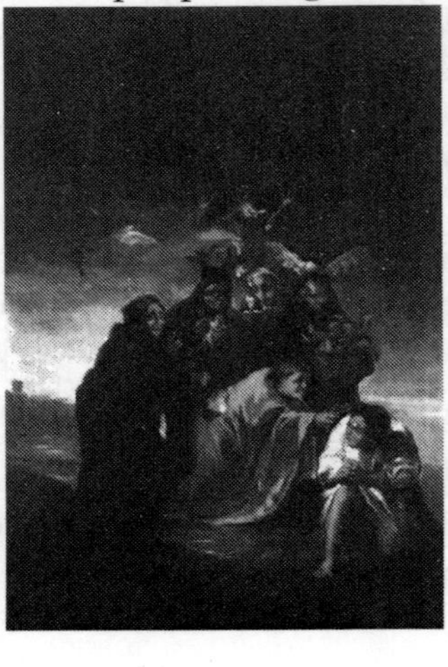

■ incremental repetition

a literary term meaning the repetition of a phrase in a poem with either minor consecutive modifications or different contexts which effect slight changes in meaning.

■ indeterminacy

the opposite of determinacy, i.e., the notion that the final meaning of a text cannot be settled once and for all, undermining an audience's certainty about such things as closure or E. D. Hirsch's tidy distinction between meaning and significance. The reasons for this are as various as the theories that make use of the concept, but none is so radical as deconstruction.

■ indeterminism

the doctrine of free will, i.e., that one is able to act as one wishes, without the constraints of determinism.

■ index

1. any of a number of devices which serve to point out or indicate, as in the index of a book, the index finger, an economic growth index, etc.

2. in Peircean semiotics, 'index' means a signifier which alludes to an absent, signified by pointing in its direction, usually by virtue of some causal connection.

■ indoctrination

to teach a doctrine, principle, etc., usually through repetition and adherence to authority, rather than a truly heuristic method.

■ induction

reasoning in which a general principle is derived from a number of specific observations. Induction states that while the available premises may not guarantee the truth of the conclusion, they may collectively suggest there is good reason to accept it.

■ indulgence or indictment

it is often difficult to determine if a representation, particularly of something a given audience finds distasteful, is shown simply for the sake of indulgence or if it is chosen to draw critical attention to some issue relating to the subject. There are no simple formulas to make this determination. Canadian censors have unwittingly drawn attention to the issue: they banned the October 1986 issue of Playboy because they interpreted an ambiguous photograph of a nude woman rolling in parachute cords as bondage. Yet feminist artists Carmen Coulombe and Persimmon Blackbridge have both made images which feature much more explicit bondage. Works which blur the line between gratification on the one hand and cries of social injustice on the other should be debated rigorously.

inexhaustibility by contrast

in A Theory of Art: Inexhaustibility by Contrast, philosopher Stephen David Ross employs certain features of ordinal theory (number theory which concerns the position of a thing in a ordered system) to explain how the meanings of an artwork can never be fully catalogued or explained, thus achieving multivocality or polysemy. Ross argues that anything that exists is located as a constituent in many orders, which is to say that it belongs to many sets or categories of things, a phenomenon he calls 'multiple locatedness'. For example, a portrait painting can belong to the hypothetical orders 'surfaces covered with paint' and 'objects hung on the wall', yet it may have little in common with certain other members of that order, e.g., 'highchair' (also a painted surface) or 'coatrack' (also suspended on the wall). The relations that the painting has to other members of its orders may be relatively stable, as in a classification of paintings according to genre. If this is the case, Ross describes the order as having integrity in a particular location, giving rise to actualities of meaning.

influence

the effect of antecedent conditions, persons, works or the like on an individual artist, as in 'Michelangelo was influenced by Jacopo della Quercia's baptismal font in Bologna.' The study of influence is at the heart of classical source analysis, but it has recently been amended substantially by the Freudian-inspired anxiety of influence.

information theory

a theory of language and, by extension, the arts, based on models of information exchange in electronic media. Simply put, the theory presents any communication as a circuit in which a sender codes a message and transmits it along a channel to a receiver, who decodes it to achieve a hypothetically complete reconstruction and, therefore, closure.

■ **informe**

Georges Bataille said that 'informe' (sometimes translated 'formless') is 'a term that serves to bring things down in the world' and that the goal of philosophy is to give a shapeless universe a 'mathematical frock coat'.

■ **in medias res**

a literary term for a narrative beginning 'in the middle of things', retracing the beginning of the story through flashbacks.

■ **innateness hypothesis**

once influential Chomskyan notion that children's ability to learn their language rapidly indicates that they are born with an innate knowledge of language's deep structure.

■ **innovation**

the introduction of something new, as in the rapid stylistic changes of the period of so-called 'heroic' modernism. Innovation, especially of an adversarial sort, was one of the cornerstones of the avant-garde. Postmodern artwriters tend to think that the novelty produced by innovation is more of an illusion than anything.

■ **inscription**

1. originally, symbols or words engraved into a surface. By extension, a written dedication or other statement in a book or on an artwork.

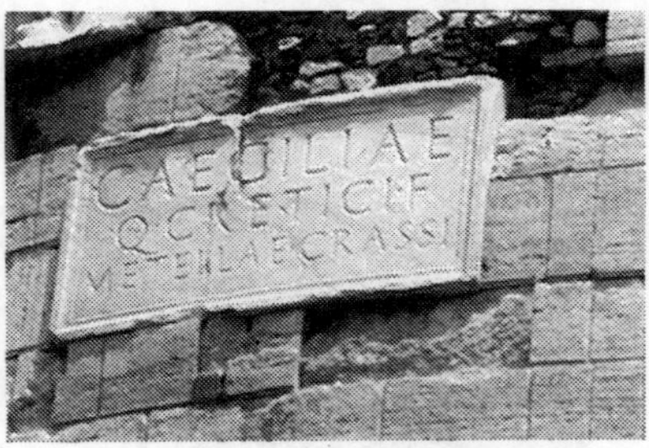

2. more recently, the way one text insinuates itself into another: this can be through a kind of appropriation, homage or imitation, as in James Joyce's Ulysses inscribed within the outlines of Homer's Odyssey or a less apparent intertextuality.

■ installation

a type of art in which a given space is redefined by the (usually) temporary arrangement therein of objects and/or materials in quasi-sculptural and/or quasi-theatrical constructions. Examples can range from traditional museum dioramas and similar arrangements of readymade articles to galleries filled with everything from topsoil to pennies to individually wrapped candies.

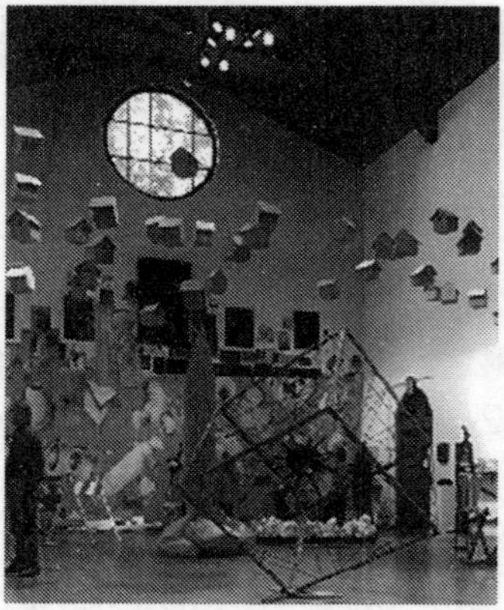

■ insufficiency

an insufficient definition is one which describes too few characteristics to differentiate the thing being defined from some other, similar thing.

■ intellectual fashion

immoderate adherence to theoretical innovation for the sake of appearances, faddishness, sycophancy and the like. The terrible seductiveness of intellectual fashion is clearly demonstrated every decade or so, when a notable figure publicly repudiates his or her earlier work.

■ intended reader

a literary term meaning the conceivable type of audience(s) for whom a text was composed. This ranges from the simple, such as a competent native speaker of the language in which the text was written, to the complex, such as a reader with a similar level of education.

■ intended viewer

see **intended reader**.

■ intensional definitions

definitions which identify the essential qualities that make something a member of a class, using genus (the larger class of things to which something belongs) and differentia (what marks off a thing from the other members of a class).

■ intentional evidence

evidence pertaining to the intentions of an author or artist in creating an artwork. Because of the intentional fallacy, however, the artwork alone cannot be considered among this evidence.

■ intentionalism

any interpretive strategy that gives priority to the intentions, whether known or inferred, of the artist.

■ intentions

the real or supposed motives of an artist in making a particular work. The idea is currently in disfavour in the critical community, largely because of the death of the author and the intentional fallacy. However, the need to know or construe an artist's intentions still seems to be strong among younger art students and the general public.

■ in(ter)determinacy

a neologism implying a contradictory state of affairs in which the different elements of an utterance help to determine each other's meaning by a process of mutual inflection, thus constraining meanings to the possibilities offered within the present terms of the utterance. At the same time, indeterminacy is always acknowledged as a possibility, even within those constraints, so closure can still be avoided.

■ intergeneric

pertaining to an artwork which belongs to more than one genre.

■ interior monologue

a literary device for the representation of the uninterrupted flow of consciousness, as in the famous Molly Bloom section of James Joyce's Ulysses. Visual art has interior monologues of a sort as well, ranging from the turbulent narrative flow of Max Ernst's Une Semaine de bonté to the agitated self-expression of Jackson Pollock's all-over paintings.

intermedia

the use of a variety of media in an interdisciplinary way. This still somewhat fashionable term was first used by Dick Higgins in late 1965 in a context describing what we would now call performance art.

internalised oppression

the processes by which oppressed groups, particularly women in patriarchal societies, accommodate their society's definition of them. Although the phrase is not always used, the idea operates in such things as the beauty myth.

interpretability

the degree to which a text, work or other thing admits of interpretation. Interpretability is an historically relative phenomenon: at one point in time, for example, it would have been taken as a matter of course that high art by definition could be interpreted with greater refinement and a greater yield in meaning than low art. In contemporary postmodern discourse, however, the interpretability of even commercial advertising, to say nothing of kitsch, is often not significantly different from that of fine art.

interpretatio excedens

a legal term designating an interpretation that is only loosely related to the evidence at hand. Subjective impressionism and all other types of criticism that affectedly read into works of art can be so described.

interpretation

standard dictionaries give 'interpretation' as the act of setting forth the meaning of something (as in explanation or clarification), the construal of meaning (as in confabulation or interpolation), the translation of material from one form into another (including that done for the purposes of computer programs) and the manner of performance (as in a particular rendering of music or drama).

interpretatio predesti-nata
a legal term designating an overly biased interpretation (i.e., one that emphasises only the evidence tending to prove something the interpreter has already decided about).

interpretatio restricta
a legal term designating a very strict interpretation (i.e., one that sticks very close to material evidence and objectively verifiable presumptions).

interpreter
one who performs an interpretation.

interpretive community
any identifiable social formation or subcomponent thereof which shares certain values or a horizon of expectations can be identified as an interpretive (or interpretative) community. An individual viewer does not merely receive an artist's meaning in the form of an unequivocal message carried along a channel. Instead, s/he "presuppose[s] the company of others who are also looking at it...[and] continually reconstructing it — a community of viewers," in the words of Michael Parsons (How We Understand Art).

interpretive ingenuity
an act of interpretation which places greater emphasis on its own cleverness, inventiveness, originality or resourcefulness than it places on the work which it interprets. Most contemporary critical modes which share as their point of departure the death of the author have some degree of interpretive ingenuity.

interpretive web
any of the several models of interpretation which attempt to be exhaustive without evoking closure, especially one which is determined to exploit all categories of con-

tent, context and form, even when contradictory results are obtained.

■ interrogation
the act of questioning someone or something. In many postmodern contexts, the term is nearly synonymous with intervention.

■ intersubjectivity
pertaining to the unfettered exchange of the contents of consciousness, conceived not as the one-way dissemination of objective knowledge but as the mutual communication of subjects' responses to experience.

■ intertext
one of the texts modifying another text in intertextuality.

■ intertextuality
term proposed by Julia Kristeva in La Révolution du langage poétique to describe the way a single work can actually consist of several texts and/or the transposition of one set of signs into another. Kristeva described it as a text conceived as a "mosaic of quotations..., [an] absorption and transformation of another text." It is a specific type of coextension in which a variety of diverse meanings overlap and interrelate within a text in ways unforeseen by its author.

■ intervention
the refusal, subversion or renegotiation of received meanings, usually because those doing the intervening believe such meanings to be enforced by political power or general consensus, which is of course determined by ideology. Intervention is standard practice in numerous manifestations of contemporary culture, from feminist revisionism to punk bricolage.

■ intolerance
inability or unwillingness to grant or to share equal rights and privileges. Both sides of the debate on political correctness accuse the other of intolerance. For example, there have been many in-

stances of hypocrisy in which one side literally shouts down the other, in spite of its own claims to freedom of expression. Oddly, even those who made the first politically correct agendas have sometimes been attacked by a second generation.

intrasignificant
in classical linguistics, relations of mutual interpretation between signs, without necessarily making reference to some external object. The idea is central to Baudrillardean thought.

intrigue
a subcategory of genre, meaning any representation placing emphasis on collusion, scheming and trickery, as in Fragonard's portrayals of the progress of courtly love.

intrinsic
inherent, innate, characteristic of a thing by its very nature. Some art historians maintain a traditional distinction between instrinsic and extrinsic approaches to the work of art. W. Eugene Kleinbauer, for example, anthologised writings on form and iconography as intrinsic, separating them from writings on psychology, society and the history of ideas as extrinsic.

intrusive narrator
a narrator who interrupts a narrative in order to offer commentaries of various sorts.

invalidity
in informal logic, an argument is invalid if its conclusion does not follow necessarily from its premises or if it lacks relevance and/or sufficiency.

irrelevance
premises which do not increase the probability of the claim they are intended to support. The classic types of contextual irrelevance are the red herring and the straw man (or straw figure). The former is an inappropriate shift in the boundaries of an issue through the introduction of an irrelevant consid-

eration, as might be the case if one alluded to Margaret Bourke-White's bank account in a discussion of her photographic composition.

■ irony

a trope in which the latent meaning is the opposite of the manifest meaning or markedly different from it. Irony is a particularly slippery trope, for an apparently bald statement of fact can be turned upside down by something as simple as a slight inflection of the voice. This is also true of imagery, although there are unequivocal instances as well. An untitled work of 1969 by Shusaku Arakawa bears the text "I have decided to leave this canvas completely blank," invoking a certain type of irony.

■ ism

1. a back formation from words with the suffix 'ism', indicating a distinctive doctrine, system, theory, etc.
2. in art history, a period designation, often but not necessarily ending in 'ism', whether that period is determined by stylistic (e.g., Impressionism), iconographical (postmodernism), chronological (Early Renaissance) or other criteria.

■ isogloss

a boundary differentiating linguistic features.

■ isomorphism

literally, isomorphism means 'different in ancestry but having the same shape'. Figuratively, practitioners of artwriting use it to mean 'different signifiers which have the same meaning (i.e., signified)'.

■ jamming

see **culture jamming**.

■ jargon

Pierre Bourdieu has argued that academic jargon, which he says imagines itself to be objective and value-free, has meanings it is not aware of and that its self-image as liberal humanism disguises its history of oppressing marginal groups.

jeu
French term for play.

jingle
dictionaries of literary terms often include 'jingle', a short, infectious verse set to music for advertising purposes, in order to distinguish it from 'literature' proper.

jouissance
the usual English translation, 'enjoyment', does not carry the sexually orgasmic connotation that the French does in addition to the idea of taking pleasure in something. In Lacanian circles, jouissance is distinguished from pleasure in that the latter indicates simply the search for psychic balance through the release of tension, whereas the former is supposed to be a perpetual state in violation of the pleasure principle. There is thus an implicit analogy drawn between demand and desire.

judicial criticism
any of several types of criticism sharing the goal of judgement of a work, as connoisseurship is thought to judge quality. The criteria that the work is supposed to meet vary widely, however.

Jungian
pertaining to the theories of Swiss psychiatrist Carl Gustav Jung.

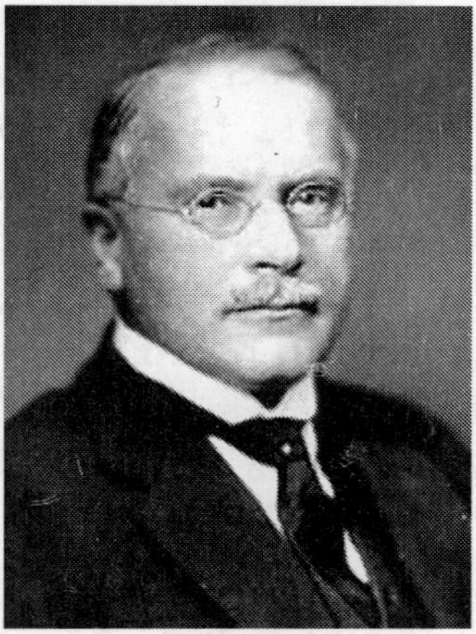

Jungian criticism
criticism influenced by Jungian ideas, principally the role of the collective unconscious in the determination of cultural behaviour. Every individual participates in two psychic streams, one personal and one supposedly sharing psychic constants with everyone else. The emphasis in practical Jungian

writing, however, often ends up on the latter of these two streams, leading some opponents to describe Jungian approaches as essentialist.

■ **juvenilia**

artworks produced during the artist's youth. In literary studies, 'juvenilia' usually implies a degree of artistic immaturity. In art history, some juvenilia is considered prodigious (i.e., produced by a prodigy, as in the case of Gianlorenzo Bernini, Michelangelo Buonarroti, John Everett Millais or Pablo Picasso).

■ **juxtaposition**

a placing of objects, images, etc., side by side. The term is particularly common in writings on Surrealism: there, because the practice was used with emphasis on the irrationality of the things juxtaposed, it sometimes seems to have an extra connotation of weirdness or inappropriateness.

■ **Kantian**

pertaining to the ideas of Immanuel Kant.

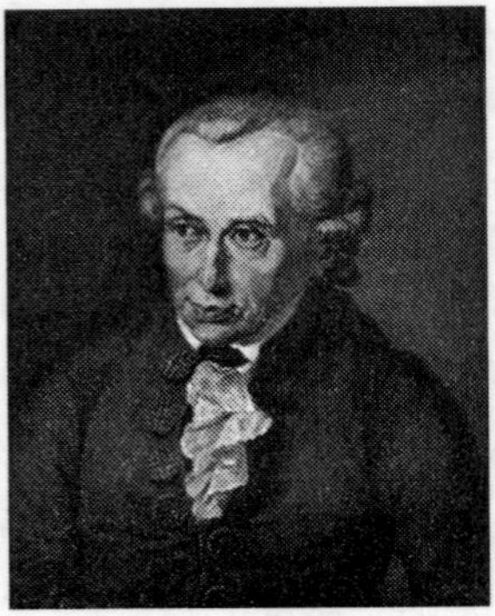

■ **kenosis**

a process of draining, evacuating, lowering, relinquishing, surrendering or yielding, as when Christ lowered Himself from divine to human form. Harold Bloom uses the term as a trope amalgamating the senses of bassesse and bathos.

■ **kitsch**

variously translated as 'artistic rubbish' or 'gaudy trash', kitsch derives from an old German word meaning 'to throw together', according to some dictionaries. The word thus means any artwork which is thrown together chiefly to satisfy popular taste, rather than to state anything of high moral value or to advance a new aesthetic.

■ Kristevan

pertaining to the ideas of French thinker Julia Kristeva, herself influenced strongly by Lacanian ideas and her followers.

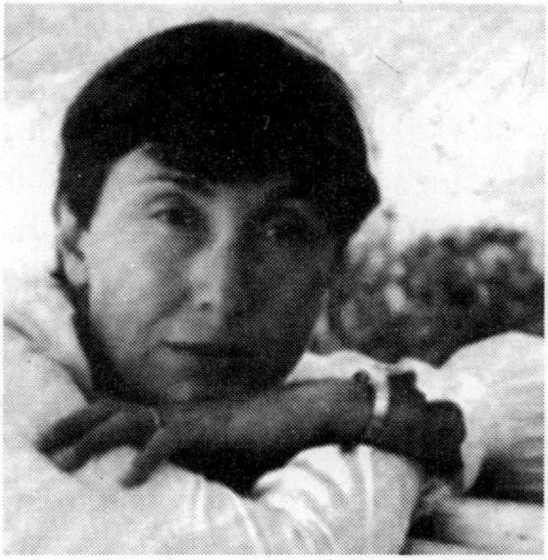

■ Lacanian

pertaining to the ideas of psychoanalyst Jacques Lacan (in écrits and particularly The Four Fundamental Concepts of Psychoanalysis) and his followers in the arts community regarding the functions of language in the construction of consciousness and unconsciousness.

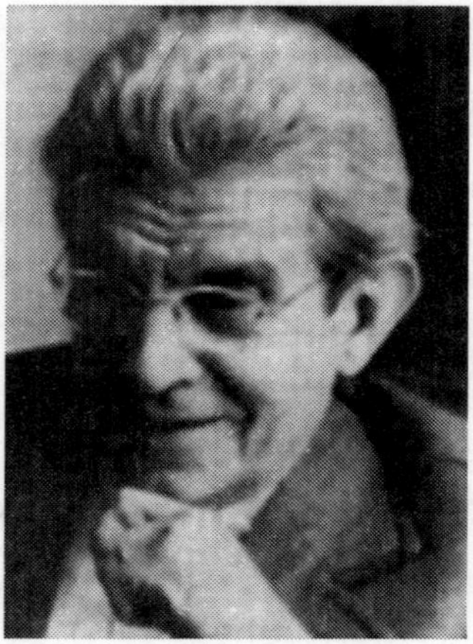

■ lack

deficiency or absence of something. In psychoanalytical contexts, this usually entails castration anxiety, but any number of other lacks have been proposed. The French ' manque' means 'lack' in most expressions except for Lacan's manque-à-être.

■ lament

in literary jargon, a poem expressing deep grief. It is usually more personal in nature than a complaint, just as Edvard Munch's various portrayals of bedside sorrow are more moving to today's sensibilities than Jacques-Louis David's Death of Socrates.

■ **lampoon**
a particularly harsh type of satire. Daumier's notorious depiction of Louis-Philippe as Gargantua is a clear example.

■ **langscape**
a neologism coined by Gaile McGregor to indicate the way conceptions of the world (formulated within language) actually alter perceptions of the world (expressed in the landscape).

■ **language**
adherents to formalism held that language and visual art were completely incompatible. For example, one of the more quotable quotes of the minimalist generation was, "If I wanted to send a message, I'd call Western Union." The implication, of course, is that mere message sending was beneath the dignity of formalist reductivism. Since the advent of postmodern thought, however, virtually every advanced discussion of art treats it as having very strong similarities with language, if not exact parallels.

■ **language-like**
see **language**.

■ **legend**
1. a specific instance, usually in the form of a short tale, of folklore. Legends often appear in visual art, as in Richard Dadd's The Fairy Feller's Master-Stroke.
2. a caption or illustrative remark superimposed on charts and maps.

■ **leipsomena**
remainders. In Derridean deconstruction, one can never account for all of the interpretive possibilities of a particular text, preventing the interpreter from invoking closure. That is, a particular metaphor, for example, can never be said to mean such and such and nothing else because "metaphor is never innocent," as Derrida said and always has some re-

mainders — some strings attached, as it were.

■ leitmotif

in literature, the reappearance of a verbal image, a concept and/or a situation to create the impression of a unifying theme. Max Ernst's frequent use of the word 'perturbation' in the captions of his La Femme 100 têtes and his frequent use of images of fingers touching eyes could be so considered.

■ lexeme

term used in some linguistics to identify the fundamental reference which underlies and thus unifies the varying inflections of a word. E.g., 'run, runs, running, ran' are variants of the lexeme 'run'. In The Conflict of Interpretations, Paul Ricoeur uses the idea to help establish the isotopy of an utterance.

■ liberal arts

from the Latin for 'work befitting a free man', as opposed to the 'vulgar arts', understood as menial trades suitable only for serfs and other undesirables. The phrase was is in use in ancient Greece, but it was systematised in the Middle Ages into the 'trivium' (grammar, rhetoric and logic) and the 'quadrivium' (arithmetic, astronomy, geometry, music). Neither the antique nor the medieval conceptions of the liberal arts held the actual practice of art-making (in whatever form) in high esteem. This only changed in the Renaissance, when the intellectual aspects of art-making were emphasised, enabling fine arts to be considered one of the humanities. Although this foregrounding of the artist's intellectuality was gradually repudiated in the Romantic era, the connection between visual art and academic or scholarly pursuit has remained strong, particularly since the rapid growth of liberal arts colleges in the 1960s.

libidinally driven
Friedrich Nietzsche once asserted that Raphael's Madonnas were the products of an overheated sexual imagination which could not find literal expression. Sigmund Freud added further momentum to this notion of unconscious motivation by describing it as a drive fuelled by the libido. In some current writing, the conception is applied to everything from the act of interpretation to relations between teachers and students.

libido
although Freud had something in mind rather broader, 'libido' is usually used to indicate the sexual instinct or drive.

licensed rebels
the conservative art critic Hilton Kramer feels that alternative galleries and artist-run centres were invented in an economic heyday which sought to give expression to the individualistic American spirit, implying that their essentially adversarial stance was once the unique characteristic of mainstream American culture. As such, they were 'licensed rebels' a notion which was once held not to be contradictory. But since these spaces were the creation and permanent wards of government patronage, their adversarial stance means that they always were a sort of 'negative cultural luxury', which American society can no longer afford to support.

limen
a threshold.

linguistics
any of a variety of scientific approaches to the study of language. Linguistics concerns itself with the use, meaning and structural relationships of words and it has had far-reaching impact on other fields ranging from anthropology to artwriting. Of particular importance are the basic Saussurean concepts employed in semiotics and their influences on

deconstruction and Lacanian thought. Also influential are the diverse Barthesian applications of linguistic ideas. These remain more popular for contemporary artwriting than Peircean ideas, despite the latter's greater applicability to pictorial signs. Also important, but very nearly ignored in artwriting, are the Chomskyan investigations of linguistic principles. Linguistics in general may be 'diachronic', studying the historical changes of language over time or 'synchronic', studying the state of language at a given time. One encounters both terms in current artwriting.

■ lisible

French for 'legible' or 'readable'. The term is problematic, since 'legibility' implies something is there to be read. Some theorists, especially those influenced by deconstruction and indeterminacy, deny that this is the case.

■ litany

a ritualistic speech, chant or petition, as in the long, formal incantations of the organised churches.

■ literacy

the ability to read and write and/or having the ability to demonstrate accomplishments, education, knowledge, etc. The idea has been transposed and disseminated across a wide variety of disciplines, but not without contradiction and complexity. Music literacy is generally understood to be the ability to read music in printed form, whereas common conceptions of visual literacy range from little more than art appreciation to more sophisticated analysis based on the principles of linguistics.

■ literal

'According to the letter', the actual, non-metaphorical or primary sense of an utterance, as opposed to a figurative expression. Taken literally, a figurative statement like 'she was on cloud nine' is immediately recognided as absurd. Strangely, visual images are often taken to be literal in spite of their figurativity. Only the most familiar conventions, like a personification of justice as a blind woman, immediately escape the literal level of meaning.

■ litotes

a subspecies of irony or understatement in which something is said by negating its opposite. In vernacular speech, for example, 'not bad' means 'good' and a more refined version of the device is common in English poetry. The conception might be of some use in discussions of indulgence or indictment. Since negation of this sort is not common in visual art, the idea is more likely to be found in the form of meiosis.

■ livret

a small handbook used to identify and explain works of art hung in academic Salons in the nineteenth century, often with much longer titles than those by which the works became known. The livret is a forerunner of the modern exhibition catalogue.

■ locale

the actual geographical and/or physical setting of a narrative, as opposed to the immaterial aspects of setting, like the protagonist's state of mind or the topos of the work. In David's Oath of the Horatii, for example, the locale is an atrium in a Roman house, whereas the setting includes the locale along with other background information like the characters' determined state of mind. The topos would be the exemplum virtutis.

■ logocentric

pertaining either to the notion that words have a necessary relation to the things they designate or to the notion that words have determinate meaning. Any worldview that considers words as objects rather than as social relations implies a certain presence hovering just behind the word itself, giving deconstruction a toehold in its struggle against logocentrism.

■ lookism
discrimination on the basis of one's appearance.

■ low art (culture)
see **high art (culture)**.

■ ludic
pertaining to play.

■ lyric
originally linked to lyric poetry, as deriving from the traditional image of the poet as a single figure expressing his or her emotions to the accompaniment of a lyre. The term is now used to describe any type of expression in words, images, movements, etc., which emphasises subjective states, marked use of the imagination and 'musical' forms.

■ macabre
the principal defining characteristic of a work emphasising the gruesome or morbid.

■ machine
deriving from the same sense of 'contrivance' that underlies 'machinery' and 'machination', certain grandiose works of (particularly academic) art that have a rather obvious allegory or other special significance are sometimes called 'machines'.

■ macrohistory
antonym of microhistory, i.e., the historical study of very broad patterns of cultural change.

■ macula
a blemish, spot or stain. Jacques Derrida uses the term as one of his many metaphors for an aporia in a text.

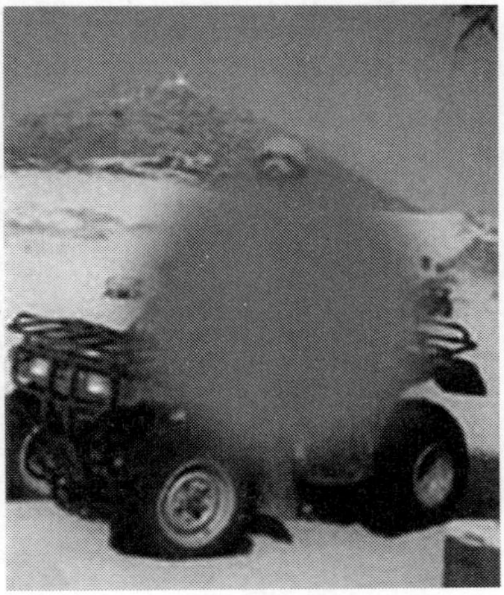

maesta
a maestà is a painting of the Madonna with Angels and Saints, the most famous of which are arguably Duccio's and Simone Martini's. The word itself means nothing more than 'majesty'.

magico-religious
the defining characteristic of art presumed to have had a ritual purpose, whether directed at spiritual ends or purely practical ones. Much paleolithic art, like the Lascaux cave paintings, is thought to have been magico-religious in order to ensure success in the hunt. Some of these practices may actually have succeeded coincidentally, rather than due to some effective communication with supernatural forces. E.g., one practice of divination in the Arctic far north was to heat deer scapulas until they cracked. The hunters would then follow the direction of the cracks, believing that the gods had shown them the way. What success they had was certainly due instead to the randomisation produced by the practice, thus ensuring that they do not exhaust the supply of game in one area.

magisterial discourse
an approximate synonym for metanarrative.

making special
the valuation of something as distinctive and exceptional. The term is directly used in ethology, which concludes that the evolutionary value of art as a human behaviour has nothing to do with expression, history, investment, meaning, etc., but has something to do with 'making special'. Exactly how this might be the case is not very clear. The concept also operates implicitly in such things as the 'is' of artistic identification.

malapropism
the erroneous use of an inappropriate word in the place of a similar but appropriate one. The term derives from Mrs. Malaprop in R. B.

Sheridan's The Rivals, who erred humorously with phrases like 'as headstrong as an allegory on the banks of the Nile'. One wonders if there is not some visual analogy to this, as in Magritte's exchange of the features of a torso for those of a face in Le Viol.

■ manifest content

the literal imagery of a dream or, by extension, of an artwork.

■ mannerism

emphasis on the manner of presentation rather than the substance of the presentation, as in the cliché 'all style and no substance'. This includes departures from normal appearance via distortion, eccentricity, exaggeration, stylisation, etc. The most immediately recogni-sable type of mannerism is characterised by abnormally elongated but nonetheless graceful figures, ranging from Parmigianino's elongated madonnas to Ingres's various odalisques, Modigliani's attenuated figures and beyond. Architectural mannerism is thought of as a playful misuse of the classical vocabulary of forms, as in the famous slipping keystones in the arches of Giuliano Romano's Palazzo del Tè. In this respect, a good deal of architectural postmodernism is mannerist.

■ manque

see **lack**.

■ manque-à-être

Lacanian term for what he called a 'want-to-be', a species of desire in which the individual wants to be the other which he perceives as lacking in himself.

■ map, mapping

maps and mapping often enter postmodern discourse in their senses of representations or detailed surveys of a particular field. Influenced by linguistics and the notion of différance, however, artwriters usually implicitly accept a dictum of general semantics: 'the map is not the territory' — i.e., the signifier is not the signified but only a representation, a social construct.

■ marginal

the opposite of central: in the margins, peripheral or non-essential. Visible minorities and other oppressed groups are often described as marginal. To make others feel less important by associating them with what one considers dispensable or superfluous is to marginalise them. A classic example is the typical exclusion of women and non-white artists from the art-historical canon.

■ marginalia

not to be confused with marginal, except in the literal sense of 'in the margins'. Marginalia is material written in the margins of a book as a running commentary by a reader. The most famous verbal example in art history is William Blake's marginalia to Sir Joshua Reynold's Discourses, wherein Blake says such things as "The following 'Discourse' is particularly Interesting to Blockheads...." Quick sketches in the nineteenth-century Salon livrets are the visual equivalent of marginalia.

■ Marxian

pertaining to the ideas of economist/sociologist Karl Marx, whose conceptions of base and superstructure, commodity fetishism, dialectic, historical materialism and ideology have been elaborated into Marxism by his many followers. Some, but not all writers maintain a very strict distinction between 'Marxian', the adjectival form of Marx and 'Marxist', pertaining to the political system subsequently embellished by followers.

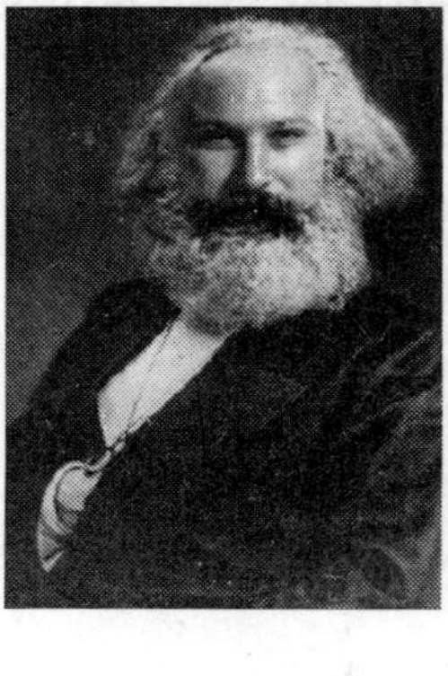

■ Marxism

any of a variety of theories and critical practices deriving from the principles of Karl Marx, Friedrich Engels and a number of followers. The chief principle is historical materialism, which, when applied to the criticism of the arts, holds that meaning is determined by the economic, historical, material and social circumstances of the era in which the work was produced, rather than by an abstract, isolated genius supposedly residing within the visionary artist. It is thus fundamentally opposed to the pseudotranshistorical. Given that artistic value is thought by Marxists to be the result of impersonal, historical determinants, it is curious that many celebrated Marxists have had a relatively traditional attitude towards the canon.

■ masculinity

the body of characteristics conventionally understood to be desirable in men, i.e. manliness, self-sacrifice, strength, virility, etc. The new masculinity argues that most of these characteristics are social constructs, which oppress men as much as patriarchy oppresses women.

■ masculism

by analogy with feminism, this word is occasionally used as a synonym for the new masculinity and therefore as the antithesis of the traditional connotations of masculinity and patriarchy.

■ masque

a subspecies of the carnivalesque, a pageant, procession or other form of spectacle involving masked figures and general revelry. Masques are thought to have begun in pagan rituals, but by the seventeenth century they had evolved into extremely expensive and highly organised entertainments for aristocratic audiences.

■ masquerade

occasionally used in the context of discussions of ideology, which operates unconsciously and therefore makes something historically specific appear to be timeless and universal. Althusser called this the 'false obviousness of everyday life' false because what is taken to be self-evident is in fact dependent upon ideological control.

mass culture
constituents of culture that evolve in similar patterns across diverse components of large societies as a consequence of common exposure to the mass media.

mass media
any form of communication reaching very large numbers of people, including movies, newspapers, radio, television and popular books and periodicals. The mass media are characteristic of complex, industrialised societies with a broad middle class.

master narrative
see **metanarrative**.

masterpiece
this word is currently thought to indicate something of such superior quality and genius that it can transcend the historical circumstances of its production and enter a supposedly universal plane of timelessness. Originally, however, it only meant the piece which a maturing student artist would make to demonstrate his competence to take on students of his own, hence becoming a master. Because of this rather obvious corruption, postmodern thought, in general, views the current meaning with strong suspicions.

master tropes
see **trope**.

material history
the historical study of the material artefacts of a culture, regardless of the identity of those objects and without significant distinctions between high art, low art and utilitarian articles. Studies of folk art are usually informed by the practices of material

history, which commonly lack the advanced vocabulary of newer art criticism.

■ materialism

the philosophy that only tangible and perceivable things, material in nature or the byproducts of such things, constitute what actually exists.

■ matriarchal aesthetic

see **matriarchy**.

■ matriarchy

literally, the rule of the mother. A social organisation in which women are the heads of their families and descent and inheritance are reckoned in the female line.

matrifocal

having the mother, maternity, matriarchy or any environment of caring, nurturing and the like as a centre of interest or focus.

■ meaning in and meaning to

phrases used by E.D. Hirsch to clarify his distinction of meaning from significance. What an image or text means for a particular audience may be less a matter of what is actually in the object than what is in the audience. 'Meaning in' is thus what the work means according to the intentions of its creator, whereas 'meaning to' is simply what it signifies to someone else, however invalid that might be.

■ meaning to

see **meaning in and meaning to**.

■ mechanistic materialism

a type of determinism which argues that causes create effects in a straightforward, predictable and irreversible fashion. In the context of political criticism, it is associated with vulgar Marxism.

■ méconnaissance

Alan Sheridan, translator of Lacan's Four Fundamental Concepts of Psycho-Analysis, put this as 'failure to recognise' or 'misconstruction' and Lacan himself aligned it with scotoma (a blind spot) in his description of the mirror stage. The gist of it is that the subject does not recognise what is Real but only what is Imaginary.

■ media

1. the plural of 'medium', the material or technique with which an artist works.
2. an abbreviation of mass media.

■ media activism

any critique of institutions or critique of representation directed at the mass media.

■ mediation

a fundamental conception in postmodernism is that nothing exists in an innocent state and that nothing can be understood objectively because everything is mediated by all manner of intervening mechanisms. Social behaviour, for example, cannot be objectively assessed because the observer is either a member of the observed group, in which case s/he is subject to the same taboos of collective consciousness or s/he is not a member of the observed group, which thus pollutes the observed behaviour. The analogy in artwriting is that the meaning of an artwork is in part determined by the institutional mechanisms, which mediate our experience of it. Native artists, for example, have drawn attention to the mediation of museums, which rip ethnographic artefacts from their original context and replace their genuine social meanings with depoliticised aesthetic ones.

■ meiosis

a type of satirical understatement, as in litotes. Goya's Family of Charles IV and The Junta of the Philippines might qualify, since both diminish their ostensible subjects (and since litotes derives from the Greek for 'diminution').

■ melodrama

a narrative which seeks primarily to evoke strong feelings in the audience by portraying sensational events in an often excessively passionate manner and usually without sincere regard for ennobling sentiment, ethics, motivation, etc. Melodrama can appear in any style, in any era. Examples are more likely to be found in the work of artists traditionally considered of second rank or lower, like J.-P.-A. Antigna's The Fire. Occasionally, artists traditionally given first rank exhibit melodramatic tendencies in works produced in the years before or after their major period, as in the turbulent early works of Cézanne.

■ memoir

a type of autobiography in which the principle interest usually resides in significant events or persons other than the author him or herself, although s/he was a witness to them.

■ meta

a prefix meaning 'above', 'after', 'beyond' or 'superior' when used in critical discourse, as in metacriticism, metafiction, metalanguage, metanarrative, metathesis, etc.

■ metacriticism

the critical examination of the premises and processes of criticism itself, independent of the particular objects of its investigations or the criticism of criticism. For example, an evaluation of a work by Niki de Saint Phalle would constitute an act of criticism. In contrast, an analysis of the premises enabling one to make such judgements in general would be part of a metacritical project. Much postmodern thought involves metacritical activity.

■ metadiscourse

see **metanarrative**.

■ meta-ethical

where ethics is popularly understood as the study of what constitutes appropriate behaviour, etc., meta-ethical thought studies the logical and other mechanisms which enable any type of ethics to be formulated. In other words, meta-ethical writing is not concerned with the specific contents of a particular branch of ethical philosophy but with the way in which that philosophy is constructed and how it relates to other constructions.

■ metafiction

also called 'surfiction', this is a type of fiction that draws attention to itself as such, severing the traditional mirror-like connections between art and life. The term is usually used of literature, as in Linda Hutcheon's 'historiographic metafiction' or historical writing which draws attention to its own fictionality. An analogous application might be made to history painting which draws attention to its own fictionality through devices like deictics or overt anachronism, as in Mark Tansey's Triumph of the New York School. An application of the same idea in history writing is called metahistory.

■ metahistory

1. generally, the philosophy of history, which considers the principles giving rise to the notion of historical progression and to the narratives which describe it.

2. more specifically, the title of a Hayden White book describing historical writing in terms analogous to those of metafiction and metanarrative. Very simply, White's thesis is that an objective history is impossible: "the very claim to have discovered...formal coherence in the historical record brings with it theories...which have ideological implications". Accordingly, postmodern metahistory must self-consciously raise questions of power and control in the act of writing.

■ metalanguage

language about language. In various types of semiotics, the language under investigation is the 'object language', while the language used to perform the investigation is the 'metalanguage'. For postmodernism influenced by relativism, the very notion of a metalanguage carries a disagreeable connotation, possibly because it seems to be an impossibility: looking at language through language might appear to be analogous to using a magnifying glass to examine itself. To achieve a state of objectivity, the metalanguage would have to stand outside history. This may not be the case, for true objectivity is not necessarily assumed in practice. For example, in a hypothetical American article about the German language, the object language would be German and the metalanguage English. There is not normally an assumption that English somehow stands outside history.

■ metalepsis

a literary term indicating an extreme type of mixed metaphor — the extreme compression of a sequence of allusions, tropes or other figures into an image or space normally too small to accommodate them all without sacrificing a degree of sense. ('Lepsis' derives from the Greek for 'seizure'.) C. Hugh Holman and William Harmon's Handbook to Literature gives as an example these lines from Yeats' 'Leda and the Swan': 'A shudder in the loins engenders there/ The broken wall, the burning roof and tower/And Agamemnon dead.' The first line alludes to Zeus raping Leda, resulting in the birth of Helen of Troy, who was the principal cause of the Trojan War alluded to in the second line. Agamemnon, mentioned in the third line, was the leader of the Greek armies in that war, but he died at the hands of his own wife Clytemnestra, who was the half-sister of Helen. The poetic seizure is that the "shudder in the loins" does not logically cause the death of Agamemnon. Because complex visual images involve the simultaneous presentation of allusions, tropes and other figures, even more intricate convulsions of meanings might take place.

metalinguistics

the investigation of the relations between language and its cultural context.

metanarrative

any narrative formed by putatively scientific, determinate knowledge. For example, a standard art history textbook is published with the tacit assumption that it is a fair and accurate representation of the truth, but it is easy to imagine how it could also be a mediation of the material it describes. (E.g., it buys into the myth of the masterpiece or it automatically excludes women's art as insufficiently influential or important). The real usefulness of the term is found in rejections of its pretension to objectivity.

metaphor

a trope consisting of a comparison without using the words 'like' or 'as', as in 'a mighty fortress is our God' or 'my love is a rose'. Generally, a metaphor poetically conveys an impression about something relatively unfamiliar, by drawing an analogy between it and something familiar. In the preceding examples, God and love are unfamiliar, but the respective impressions of strong/inviolable/protective and beautiful-but-short-lived/sweet-but-thorny are effectively conveyed.

metaphoricity

the state or condition of being metaphor.

metaphysical

pertaining to metaphysics, originally the section of Aristotle's writings that came after (meta) his discussions of the physical world (the physics) for the purpose of discussing such things as the ultimate nature of existence. As a result, any branch of philosophy that deals with something beyond verifiable physical experience, like the soul or the existence of God, is metaphysical. For most postmodern thinkers, 'metaphysical' is a term of opprobrium, as in metaphysics of presence.

■ **metaphysical realism**
see **realism**.

■ **metaphysics of presence**
deconstruction argues that certainty about determinate meaning is an impossibility founded upon the unverifiable notion that there is some sort of absolute ground of signification. Practitioners of deconstruction see this hope for a guarantee of meaning as utopian and metaphysical. Since presence indicates the hypothetical guarantor, 'metaphysics of presence' simply means the delusion that words are objects and that they have stable meaning, instead of the absence and indeterminacy recognised by deconstruction or the unstable social relations studied by Marxism and feminism.

■ **metathesis**
transposition, as in the switching of sounds in the pronunciation of a word, as in 'aks' for 'ask', 'nucular' for 'nuclear' or 'purdy' for 'pretty'. Dada collages, like Hoch's Cut with the Kitchen Knife, often involve metathetical elements — body parts switched within a figure (like an eye for a head), body parts switched between figures (like a baby with a beard) and body parts transposed with the parts of the machinery the figures are using.

■ **methodolatry**
feminist philosopher and theologian Mary Daly uses the word 'methodolatry' to denote an idolatrous worship of supposedly objective methodologies leading towards determinacy. As such, it rejects scientific disinterestedness and intellectual neutrality.

■ **methodology**
a system of methods, principles, rules, etc., organising

an inquiry and guiding the practitioner as to the appropriate means of carrying out an analysis, evaluation, investigation, etc. Methodology itself does not connote any particular sort of approach in criticism, but some feel the conception, in general, has a connotation of scientificity which they find disagreeable.

■ metonymic skid

Barthesian image of the way in which any utterance can generate a hypothetically infinite number of connotations by way of metonymy. A classic piece of writing supposedly works by placing limitations on the range of the metonymic skid, whereas many modern works do not bother to do so.

■ metonymy

a trope in which the literal name of the thing meant is replaced by the name of another thing with which it is closely associated, as when 'What is the word from the throne?' means 'what does the king or queen have to say about such and such?' In visual images, metonyms can be as simple as the use of an attribute, as a crown of thorns signifies Christ when He is Himself absent.

■ microhistory

the historical study of very minute patterns of cultural change.

■ milieu

synonym for context, particularly that of the secondary sort.

■ mimesis

mimesis is a species of imitation, although the word has specialised uses ensuring that it is not a straightforward synonym. Mimesis is the enactment of the elements of a text as opposed to the imagination of them. In other words, the showing of things as opposed to the telling of things. An actor performing a play engages the text mimetically, whereas a reader of a play engages it diegetically.

■ **mimetic theory**

any theory stressing the artwork as an unmediated representation or close imitation of reality. Mimetic theory is challenged in the thinking of Michael Riffaterre (Semiotics of Poetry). In such a theory, the elements of the work are considered literal, since they purport to be in actuality what they appear to be. Any stress on figurative meaning is, therefore by definition, a shift from mimesis to semiosis.

■ **mimicry**

occasionally used as a near synonym for any of camouflage, imitation or simulation, all of which have slightly different senses.

■ **mind**

see **mind-body problem**.

■ **mind-body problem**

the traditional metaphysical problem of how the mind and body are related to one another, of what respective substances they are comprised, of how consciousness relates to matter, of how something incorporeal like consciousness can cause something physical like the body to perform an act, etc.

■ **mind-set**

an inclination or disposition. In traditional art history, mind-sets are characterisations of the disposition towards art of a whole society defined usually by geographical or temporal parameters. For example, ancient Egyptian art is thought to be conceptual, whereas later nineteenth-century art is thought to be perceptual. The most frequently cited mind-sets are 'emotive' (determined by the desire to express things passionately, leading to distortions of forms, as in German art from the Gothic Roettgen Pietà through Grünewald's Isenheim Altarpiece to early modern expressionism), 'perceptual' (determined by the desire to transcribe natural appearance, as from Giovanni Bellini's Esctacy of St. Francis to the photo-realism of the contemporary world), 'rational' (particularly common in periods with classical tendencies, like ancient Greek art) and 'ritualistic' (as in magico-religious art).

■ **mise-en-scene**
in theatre and film, the stage setting, including all props, lighting effects, costumes, etc., but excluding the narrative proper. The mise-en-scène of David's Lictors Bringing Brutus the Bodies of His Dead Sons would thus include the antique costumes and furniture which determine the setting, the light falling on the women as opposed to the shadow enshrouding the father, the general disposition of the Doric columns both to provide rational spaces for the figures but also to separate the functions they serve within the narrative, etc. Mise-en-scène is especially critical in film studies, where it implies the orchestration of all the seen elements, with special reference to composition, visual weights, the function of the frame and staged movements within the scene.

■ **misandry**
hatred of men.

■ **misogyny**
hatred of women.

■ **misology**
hatred of reason.

■ **misprision**
1. misunderstanding.
2. violation of official duty by one in office.
3. sedition or contempt, as in contempt of court. To some degree, these senses are all embodied in the use of 'misprision' in contemporary literary discourse, which derives from Harold Bloom.

■ **misreading**
Harold Bloom suggests that because of indeterminacy, we can never be entirely certain that a given reading of a text is the correct one. As a result, all readings are misreadings (or misprisions). He does allow, however, that

some misreadings might be more compelling than others.

mixed metaphor

a figure in which two metaphors are illogically or incongruously combined, often producing an unexpectedly humorous or grotesque effect, as in 'Napoleon III hastened to put the ship of state back on its feet.' While mixed metaphors are easiest to recognise in their verbal form, they can be found in visual images, especially those which employ a richly metaphorical iconography from the outset, as in seventeenth century still-life painting or Surrealist images.

mobile

a usually spidery construction made of objects hung on vertical strings from various points on horizontal wire arms so that it is both balanced and capable of free movement.

modelling

in two dimensional work, modelling is a means to create the effect of light on a virtual three-dimensional form by manipulating the values of light, shadow and colour. In three-dimensional work, modelling refers to the additive method, i.e. building up a form by progressively shaping a malleable material like clay.

monoculturalism

occasionally used as an antonym of multiculturalism, i.e., the practice of making one's own culture central and ignoring or oppressing all others. Typically, a Eurocentric person is thought to practice a type of monoculturalism.

morpheme

a meaningful linguistic unit that contains no smaller meaningful parts. A morpheme may exist in a free state, as in the word 'box' or it may be bound to another unit, as the 'es' of 'boxes'.

moving equilibrium

see **hegemony**.

■ **multimodal**

using more than one mode of critical, historical or other discourse.

■ **multiple drafts**

a recent theory about the structure of consciousness, promulgated by Daniel Dennett in Consciousness Explained.

■ **museology**

the study of the history, functions and classification of types of museums, as well as their roles in society, their systems for research, conservation, education and organisation and their relationships with their physical and social environments.

■ **museum**

a non-profit, permanent institution in the service of society and of its development and open to the public, which acquires, conserves, researches, communicates and exhibits for the purposes of study, education and enjoyment, material evidence of man and his environment.

■ **myopia**

nearsightedness. Art-for-art's-sake had a specific historical moment — a finite lifespan and currency. So does everything else, including postmodernism and every traditional approach. Those who cannot 'see' beyond their immediate moment suffer from myopia.

■ **mystory**

in Ulmer's teletheory, a method of teaching that acknowledges subjectivity and a postmodernist distrust of authority and metanarratives.

■ **myth**

in addition to the usual connotations of fable, folklore, legends, superstitions, etc., 'myth' has taken on several implications in postmodern thought. For example, in the work of Roland Barthes, myth is the result of ideology's dehistoricising of cultural phenomena, of lifting them out of their historical specificity, as in timelessness. All forms of culture, both the putatively high and low, are subject to a process which disguises the ideological character of the phenomena so that they appear natural and commonsensical. The meanings of these phenomena are precisely not natural, however, for they are imposed by particular sectors of the population who maintain power by duping disempowered sectors into thinking that the meanings are universal. Innumerable examples could be cited, but arguably the most basic one in artwriting is the canon of masterpieces, which in this view is little more than a celebration of empowered patrons of the past for their taste and economic success. The unraveling of this state of affairs is intervention.

■ mythic criticism

criticism which chooses to search for a text's formative influences and constitutive elements in the realm of myth.

■ mythopoeia

a deliberate creation of myth by aping archetypes and other folkloric characteristics. It can be found in the work of many artists of a generically Romantic sensibility, ranging from William Blake's rewriting of the Old Testament to Leonora Carrington's Jungian-inspired depictions of a prelapsarian world. Mythopoeia is considered a characteristic of self-conscious cultures and is therefore almost invariably Eurocentric.

■ name

in his Principles of Semantics (1957), Stephen Ullman uses the word 'name' in a sense analogous to signifier, while Ullman's 'sense' corresponds to signified.

■ name-of-the-father

English translation of the Lacanian expression nom-du-père, by which Lacan meant any allusion to the father as he appears in the Symbolic realm. Whereas the Real father is simply a biological entity and the Imaginary father is the paternal imago (the idealised image of the father, with ramifications ranging from the anxiety of influence to castration), the symbolic father is the psychological principle of father as authority or Law, something to which the subject binds himself.

■ narration

one of the four classic types of written composition, the others being argumentation, description and exposition. The function of narration is to deliver a narrative, although it may also include descriptive or other elements that are not narrative proper. In a simplistic distinction, the narrative is comprised of the events of a story, whereas the narration consists of the way(s) in which the story is presented, ranging from the implied author's tone to such things as the actual order of events.

■ narrative

a story of events and experiences.

■ narrative analysis

critical writing aimed at narrative and/or narration. It has become fashionable to apply the principles of narrative analysis to visual images.

■ narrativity

the state of having a narrative, the storytelling character of a text.

■ naturalism

the representation of something in a manner thought to be consistent with natural appearance, as opposed to stylisation.

■ nature

supposedly the opposite of culture, i.e., the world and all its phenomena as they exist without human intervention. However, since the boundaries of 'human intervention' have changed over the centuries, recent writers suggest that 'nature' itself is a cultural construct.

■ negative theology

in his famous essay 'The Work of Art in the Age of Mechanical Reproduction', Walter Benjamin argued that the traditional art-world was essentially ritualistic and functioned by distancing society at large from works of art by emphasising their ostensible uniqueness and aura. Benjamin saw the advent of photomechanical reproduction as coincident with the rise of socialism, leading to a more democratic consumption of imagery. This presumably threatened the art-world elite, who responded by proclaiming the existence of a 'pure' art which had no social function and no categorisable content. This was the famous nineteenth century doctrine of art for art's sake. Benjamin characterised this move as a deliberate act of cultural mystification, which he further described as a 'negative theology', that is, as a kind of ritual fantasy (i.e., a theology) determined by what the object is not, rather than what it is.

■ new new criticism

term sometimes employed to indicate deconstruction and to characterise it simply as a fashionable alternative to new criticism, which was itself once a fashionable alternative to something else.

■ new historicism

where the older historicisms tended to emphasise broader patterns of historical change, the new historicism places greater stress on economic, ideological, political and social phenomena in the interpretation of culture.

■ noise

1. in information theory, any sort of interference between the sender of a message and its receiver.

2. in informal logic, any material not relevant to the matter under investigation.

3. in the work of some sociologically inclined writers, an intervention or challenge to a dominant symbolic order.

■ nom-du-père

see **name-of-the-father**.

non-objective
without representation, arrangements of ostensibly autonomous formal features which make no reference to something else by virtue of resemblance.

non-representational
see **non-objective**.

novelty
conventionally, a state of newness and/or the essentially transitory amusement value of something which is novel. Since much of what historically has constituted the avant-garde has depended upon novelty, might it be legitimate to assert that one of the unexplored ramifications of avant-gardism is a certain recreational triviality?

object
something to which action or thought is directed, therefore usually conceived as subhuman, unreflective and passive, in contrast to the active subject. It is common, for example, for feminist criticism to describe a female nude as the object of the male gaze, as in Alexandre Cabanel's Birth of Venus (1863). Such figures are thus oppressed. When the female figure exhibits a less passive personality, as in Manet's Olympia (1863), she is sometimes described as a subject, at least with respect to the single issue of her gaze.

object language
see **translation**.

objectification
the process of turning something into an object. The term is very commonly used to describe the dehumanising oppression of women, visible minorities and other marginalised groups.

occasionalism
Nicolas Malebranche wondered how it was that the mind, composed of a substance fundamentally different from matter, could still have an effect on matter in the form of the body, as in the making of a gesture with the arm. He concluded that

the mind is not the true cause of the movement, but only the occasional cause (i.e., the cause on this occasion). The gesture's true cause was willed in the mind of God. This belief became known as occasionalism. The idea is admittedly rare in artwriting.

■ oceanic feeling

Adrian Stokes used this term in his own voluminous artwritings influenced by psychoanalytical criticism. It is natural, he argued, for both artist and audience to have emotional deficits which can only be gratified by a replacement for the maternal breast, which once gave generalised feelings of satisfaction, security and comfort to the relatively unindividualised (i.e., 'oceanic') infant. The presumption is that the function and affect of art are compensatory in similar ways. A more sociological spin on the basic idea can be found in participation mystique.

■ octoberists

term occasionally used of contributors to the influential journal October, which has had a pronounced tendency to post-structuralism and the like.

■ oedipus complex

the classic Freudian model of psychic development in which the male loves the mother and endeavours to slay his father, his rival for her affections. This tired paradigm, virtually a cliché, can be found in nearly all psychoanalytic criticism, the subjects of which run the gamut from Michelangelo to modernism. It is particularly common in studies of artists who were consciously aware of Freud's writing, as in the case of the Surrealists.

■ open

term used by Martin Heidegger in The Origin of the Work of Art to indicate a hypothetical space opened by a work of art where beings can come into contact with Being to achieve authenticity. Any artist whose work is routinely described in more or less existentialist terms will ostensibly provide such a space.

■ opening

in The Conflict of Interpretations, Paul Ricoeur characterises the moment at which symbolism moves towards something other than itself, i.e., the point at which its signifiers become signifieds, as its 'opening'. He further explains that this is the point at which language is 'saying', i.e., it ceases to be merely a set of noises and structures and refers to the world around it, which Ricoeur calls 'the equivocalness of being'.

■ oppression

usually defined as the unjust exercise of authority or power over another, oppression in art is usually a matter of content, as in simple illustrations of instances of oppression or somewhat more complex situations in which entire cultural groups are maligned in some more oblique way by the attitudes behind certain types of representation.

■ order

within current artwriting there are two more specific and quite distinct meanings of order: the first is traditional, referring to the architectural orders, that is, the arrangements of building components with special reference to the relations between columns and entablatures on the fronts of important classical structures. Historians usually identify as the most foundational five basic orders, the Tuscan, Doric, Ionic, Corinthian and Composite orders, each with certain identifying details and proportions, but there are numerous variations.

■ ordinal theory

mathematical theory which concerns numbers indicating relative position in an ordered series, as in 'first' or 'thirteenth'.

organic

sense 1: possessing the qualities of a naturally occurring organism or phenomenon, especially one conceived as experiencing its natural development without human intervention (for example, without chemical fertilisers, pesticides or growth hormones). Sense 2: possessing aesthetic characteristics like those of a naturally occurring organism or phenomenon, like organic lines and shapes (as opposed to geometric ones, which possess aesthetic characteristics apparently due to human intervention).

orientalism

the title of a 1994 book by Edward Said, in which he argues that the culture of the middle east (i.e., the Orient) is misrepresented by Eurocentrism because the west displaces what it does not like about itself onto the east. For example, western artists depicted exotic women of the harem so they could avoid projecting their fantasies onto the bodies of their mothers, sisters and daughters. The implications of this are enormous for studies of colonialism and imperialism.

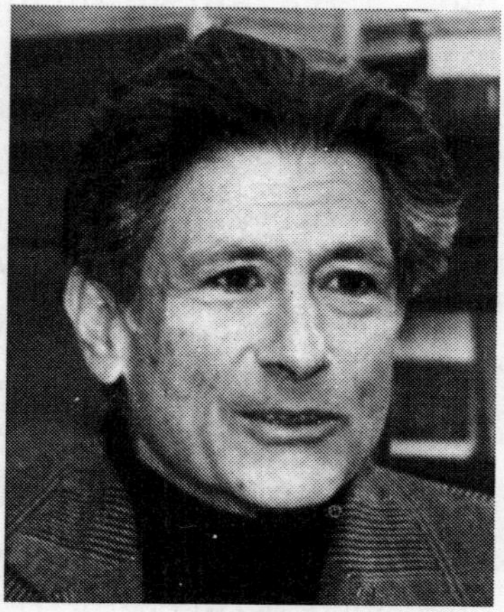

Edward Said

orthodoxy

ideas receptive to or in agreement with established doctrine or received opinion. Superficially, much postmodern thought has achieved this status in popular culture. For example, the notion that works of art have different meanings for different spectators, has almost completely replaced any idea that the author could have had something fairly specific in mind.

■ other

Simone de Beauvoir's The Second Sex appears to have been the first reference to women as 'other', so inherently different from men that men have intentionally marginalised what seems alien to them and thus failed to do justice to women in their representations. In some sources, the term has lost this gender specificity, but it has taken on added connotations deriving particularly from Lacan and Julia Kristeva. Lacan himself distinguished between the object petit a, a simple object of desire, as in the case of a one individual desiring another and what he called the grand Autre (sometimes translated 'the capital Other'), which he defined as the place of speech and therefore of desire operating within the symbolic. In other words, 'other' simply means dissimilar, excluded, opposite, while 'Other' means the more abstruse region of the pure signifier. Although neither of these terms necessarily denote women, some subsequent writers persist in using 'Other' to refer to women from the viewpoint of patriarchy.

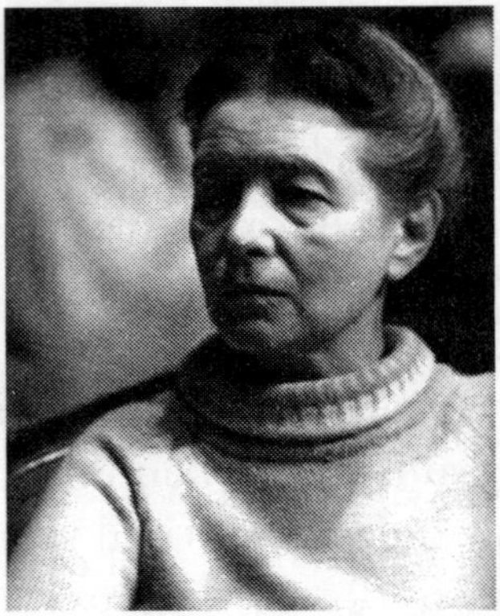

Sincon de Beauvoir

■ paean

a joyous song (hymn or analogous thing) for praising, giving thanks or tribute or celebrating triumph.

■ pageant

any of various sorts of temporary exhibitions with processions, perfomances, music and dance, colourful costumes and the like. Pageants and pageantry are fairly frequently represented in visual art of earlier centuries and some artists were also well-known for creating them (e.g., Gianlorenzo Bernini).

■ painterly

Heinrich Wölfflin's term for any formal element or compositional principle which draws attention to the characteristic sensuous traits of paint, like fluidity, looseness, impasto, scumbling, texture and so on. By analogy, even a drawing or a photograph can be painterly. Painterly works are often conventionally understood to be more impassioned than linear ones, which are associated with reason and deliberation.

■ palimpsest

a manuscript illumination or similar inscribed surface which has been erased and repainted or otherwise used more than once, so that occasionally layers of what is beneath will show through and blend or interfere with the most recent image on the surface.

■ palimpsestablishment

because it can have multiple meanings, the word 'palimpsest' is sometimes used to signify indeterminacy. But a real palimpsest is limited to those images that actually appear there. That is, a palimpsest might have commingled images of, say, a good shepherd, a pastoral scene and a classical myth. What is actually in the image establishes certain boundaries of interpretation. Within these restrictions one can still produce a bewildering variety of interpretation, depending upon the quantity and kinds of contextual information adduced.

■ palinode

a retraction of something previously said, often in poetic form.

■ painting

any of a variety of works of art made by applying paint on a surface. There is a wide variety of types of paint media, surfaces, application tools and techniques and aesthetic preoccupations. Paint media, for example, include acrylic, body colour, casein, enamel, encaustic, fresco, gouache, ink, lacquer, oil, pastel, tempera, watercolour and any number of natural alternatives from blood to elephant dung. Surfaces include animal hides, architectural features, canvas, cardboard, cotton, felt, paper, silk, wood panels, various types of natural surfaces like rock faces and cave walls and various types of three-dimensional surfaces, as in combine painting, sculpto-peinture and other forms of installation and multimedia work. Application tools and techniques include airbrush, brush, dry brush, palette knife, pen, etc. The sky's the limit for aesthetic preoccupations, since even a brief list here would constitute a summary of much of the entire history of art.

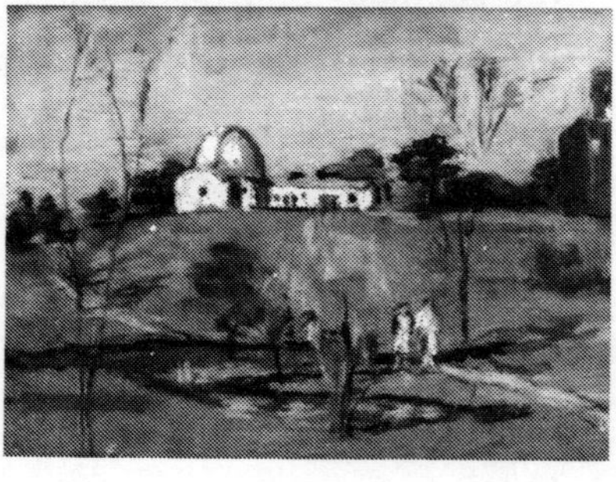

■ **panegyric**
formal praise in an elaborate or grave manner, as in a eulogy.

■ **panel**
see **painting**.

■ **panoptic**
something which provides a comprehensive or panoramic view is said to be panoptic. Jeremy Bentham's Panopticon was a model for an ideal prison in which a minimum number of guards could observe a maximum number of prisoners by virtue of having a panoptic view of the goings-on. Michel Foucault appropriated the idea as a metaphor for the scientific point of view, which can supposedly survey everything objectively.

■ **panoramic**
pertaining to a panorama, i.e., an unobstructed view in every direction. Figuratively, then, 'panoramic' indicates comprehensiveness or thoroughness in a presentation of a subject. By extension it can mean any of several types of

visual presentations that endeavour to represent an unobstructed view, as in a panoramic photograph or an enormous painting in which a seemingly endless vista is literally unrolled before an audience, as in certain pre-twentieth-century entertainments.

■ paralinguistic

a paralinguistic shift is a matter of the way form affects meaning: If one changes the delivery of a word or image (that is, the signifier), one can produce a corresponding change in the meaning of the word or image (that is, the signified). Like tropes, these shifts can be conventional, evoking an immediate, intuitive response: For example, everyone spontaneously recognises the difference between the look, sound and meaning of 'fire' and 'FIIIRRRRE!!!' Like tropes, these shifts can also be invented for expressive, aesthetic purposes, as in expressionism.

■ parent culture

a euphemism for the dominant portion of a culture.

■ parentheses

a postmodern tactic to reveal the hidden agenda of putatively neutral words. Common examples include '(cult)ure' (indicating that culture is in some respects an expression of the symbolic fetishism of cult-worship), 'imag(in)ing' (to conflate something akin to aimless day-dreaming with the deliberate construction of ideology) and so on.

■ parody

an imitation of the form or content of a prior artwork, either for comic effect or to ridicule it or its author. Originally, parody could be quickly recognised because of a marked tendency towards caricature. The famous cartoons poking fun at Courbet, Manet and others in magazines like Charivari are obvious examples. In contemporary discourse, parody is a more serious affair, usually aimed at critiquing or undermining the tacit assumptions of, say, patriarchy or late capitalism.

participation mystique

immersion of the individual self in the mystical participation, in the collective identity of a culture, usually one that is non-European in origin and practices. The idea crops up in anthropology, ethology, sociology, etc. and it plays a role in Jung's collective unconscious and visionary mode of artistic creation.

particularism

in 'Multiculturalism: E Pluribus Plures' (in The American Scholar), Dianne Ravitch divides multiculturalism into two camps, the pluralists and the particularists. The former seek a richer common culture by including marginal groups in the existing historical narrative, with appropriate modifications. The particularists' goal is separate self-fulfilment through the raising of self-esteem, ethnic pride and the like. Among other things, Ravitch sees particularism as a wrong-headed assertion that blacks or women can only achieve if taught by blacks or women. Accordingly, she concludes that it is both deterministic and filiopietistic.

passe-partout

a matte. Used metaphorically in Derrida's Truth in Painting.

pathography

Freud used this term to characterise his investigation of the unconscious motivations of Leonardo da Vinci's art. E. H. Spitz (in Art and Psyche) has suggested that the term implies that psychoanalytic criticism is necessarily preoccupied with works of art as symptoms of suffering, if not overt mental illness.

pathosformel

Aby Warburg thought that specific historical periods were characterised by coherent clusters of perceptions and feelings, as in, for example, Renaissance classicism. The expression of these perceptions and feelings demanded a certain consistency of formal approach. Warburg thought he could identify principles of configuration which he called pathosformel, which might be translated loosely as 'forms or formulas of emotional style', running through many different arts and giving expression to a wide variety of cultural preoccupations, ranging from folklore to religion.

■ patriarchy

literally, the rule of the father. A social organisation in which men are the heads of their families and descent and inheritance are reckoned in the male line. Feminism, in characterising patriarchy more generally as officially sanctioned male dominance, sees it as the root of all evil. Proponents of the new masculinity argue that feminism is right in seeing patriarchy as oppressive but that it is wrong in defining it as the universal privileging of men. A simple example is that men, historically, were drafted into the army and women were not. A more balanced view is probably that industrialised society suffers from epidemic bisexism.

■ pediment

the uppermost portion of a principal architectural facade, usually triangular, but sometimes semicircular, broken, and/or curved or the imitation of the same as a decorative motif over windows, doors and some furniture components.

■ Peircean

pertaining to the semiotics of Charles Sanders Peirce.

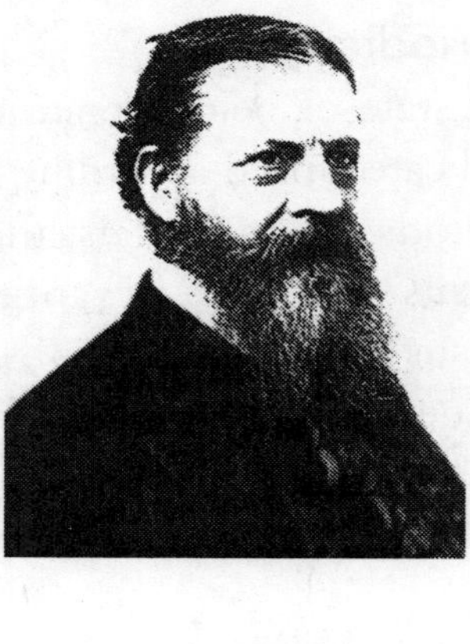

perception
the neurological processes by which sensory stimuli are recognised and assigned simple meanings.

perceptual
concerning the faculty of perception.

perceptualism
a notion appearing in the writings of Norman Bryson describing the uncritical reception of realism as optical (i.e., perceptual) truth, instead of as a meaning-bearing construction which is therefore subject to the inflections of social values. That is, when confronted with a realist image, unreflective viewers think of what is depicted only that 'it is', rather than 'it means'.

periodicity
the state of being organised and categorised according to periods, as in Renaissance versus Baroque, Byzantine versus Modern and so on. Since any such scheme streamlines, homogenises and ignores or downplays difference, much interesting material is lost. This is one of the fundamental complaints against the canon.

perruque
a French idiomatic expression meaning the work one does for oneself in the guise of work done for an employer, as when one photocopies personal material on the office account or the like. In The Practice of Everyday Life, Michel de Certeau construes the idea as a socio-cultural trope of sorts, in which the socially weak (e.g., those who must work for others) make use of the socially strong (e.g., the bosses) by carving out an independent domain within the circumstances imposed upon them from above.

personification
the conventional representation of an abstract quality by a concrete thing, usually a person with identifiable attributes. Familiar examples are Justice (a blindfolded woman holding scales) and

Liberty (a woman wearing a diadem and holding a torch aloft). In visual art, such representations have been codified for centuries. At one time, an artist who needed to know how to represent something abstract like 'knowledge' or 'charity' could turn to visual dictionaries, so to speak, like Cesare Ripa's Iconologia, which would give straightforward guidelines to follow.

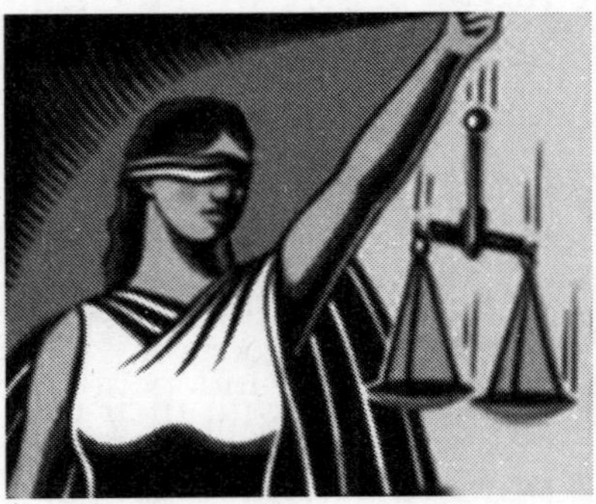

■ phallocentric

any of several self-indulgent tendencies which describe male characteristics as central and female ones as marginal. Anything which foregrounds a putatively essential masculine or patriarchal principle can be considered phallocentric.

■ phallogeneric

the sexist use of gender-specific nouns and pronouns to refer to generic humanity. For example, Montréal's Expo '67 had as its theme 'Man and His World', even though it was supposed to mean men and women collectively.

■ phoneme

in linguistics, the smallest sound, meaningless in itself, capable of indicating a difference in meaning between two morphemes. The word 'dog' differs from 'cog' by virtue of a change of the phoneme 'd' to 'c'. One of the problems of early visual semiotics was to determine what constituted a visual counterpart to a phoneme.

■ phonocentric

giving priority to the principles underlying verbal language when attempting to theorise about the very different nature of visual language.

■ **phonology**

the study of language in terms of the relationships between phonemes. Phonology can be directed at segmental features (the segments of phonemes, like consonants, vowels, syllables) or suprasegmental features.

■ **photocollage**

a collage made chiefly of photographic materials. The Berlin Dada group were especially renowned for this technique, with notable examples in the works of Hannah Höch, John Heartfield, George Grosz and many others.

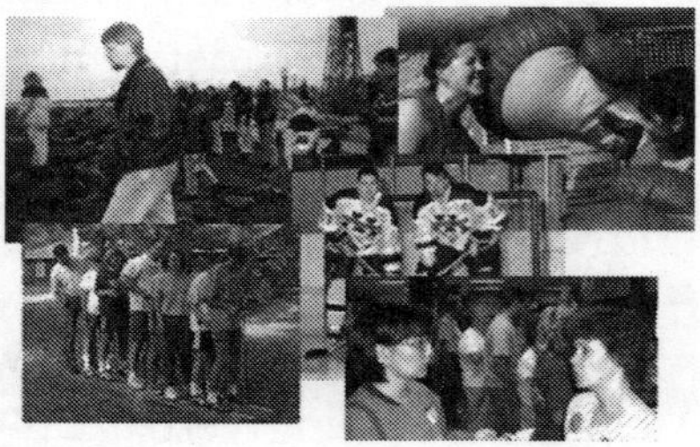

■ **photography**

the underlying principle of photography, that light could pass through a pinhole and be projected upon the other side of a darkened box, predates the mechanical means of modern photography by thousands of years. The first practical instrument to resemble a modern camera was the camera obscura (literally, an 'obscure' or 'darkened chamber'), a contraption which allowed an image to be transferred by means of a lens fitted over the hole, to a sheet of paper suspended on the other side of the chamber, where the image could be then be traced with some precision. These were available in the seventeenth century and some scholars believe Jan Vermeer may have been familiar with their use.

■ **photomontage**

a mixing of imagery through means peculiar to photography to achieve collage-like effects, not always precisely distinguished from photocollage.

■ **plaisir**

French for pleasure.

plastic

'plastic' does not mean polymer, in an artwriting context. It simply means that which can be moulded or modelled. Typically, it refers to sculptural works, especially in the German tradition, but in some contexts it means any type of visual art, before the era of photographic and electronic imagery, especially if it has 3D properties. Nothing more obscure than that.

plausibility

in Philosophy Looks at the Arts, Joseph Margolis replaces the closure and determinacy of right and wrong interpretations with the more flexible notion of plausibility. The criteria include such things as whether a conclusion is reasonable or unreasonable, appropriate or inappropriate and the like. The process of rendering interpretation more flexible consists in part of exposure to a wide variety of modes.

pleasure

see **jouissance**.

plein air

plein air simply means that the artist painted outside, literally 'in empty (or open) air', instead of in the studio.

pluralism

1. a near synonym of multiculturalism, which entails a lack of discrimination on the basis of ethnicity, gender, sexual preference, creed, class and the like.

2. in artwriting, the term is also used simply to describe the late 1960s to the 1980s, when no one style predominated and a variety of options was seen as a sign of cultural health and diversity.

political unconscious

along with many other postmodern writers, Fredric Jameson feels that an audience never encounters a text innocently, as a unique, unmediated thing. Texts appear instead as the always-already-read, something composed by a writer in response to previous texts, something discovered by a reader only through layers of previous interpretations or through inherited habits and traditions of reading. Any interpretation thus constructed is inherently ideological, but since readers are usually unaware of the operations of ideology in their habits of mind, the term 'political unconscious' is apt.

■ **politics of identity**

an umbrella term for political and/or critical agitation by specific social groups, including black nationalism, women's rights, gay and lesbian liberation, diverse ethnic revivals and so on.

■ **politics of interpretation**

an umbrella term for a variety of types of critique of the act of interpretation as a thinly-veiled ideological activity.

■ **politics of the textbook**

an umbrella term for a variety of types of critique of the textbook writing and publishing as thinly-veiled ideological activities.

■ **polysemy**

from the Greek for 'many signs', the hypothetically infinite range of meanings which results when determinacy is replaced by indeterminacy. The term has become so commonplace that it is impossible to attribute to a particular writer.

■ **positive**

see **photography**.

■ **post hoc, ergo propter hoc**

latin for 'after this, therefore on account of it'. It is a common error in argument similar to the genetic fallacy. That one thing habitually follows another thing does not ensure that the latter caused the former. A specific application of the principle is Hume's constant conjunction.

■ **postcolonial**

characterising a society moving away from cultural, economic, psychological, social and other dependence on the subordination of another social group.

■ **postindustrial**

characterising a society moving from economic dependence on heavy manufacturing (and its concomitant problems, like waste and pollution) to one more interested in information exchange, recycling, cultural democracy and a number of related things.

■ **postmodernism**

it is something of a gross oversimplification, considering that modernism and postmodernism are difficult concepts circulating in disputed territory, but it is safe to say at least that modernism tended to have faith in the perfectibility of mankind through technology and rationalistic planning. It is now felt that these were instruments of white European males interested only in maintaining their own hegemony, so the result was a certain homogeneity which disallowed cultural differences. Art which seemed to illustrate, foster or otherwise exemplify values like faith in perfectibility and rationalism was modernist art. In contrast, today's emphasis on the cultures of women, peoples of colour and gays and lesbians might be seen as postmodernist by default.

■ **potboiler**

formulaic works of art produced cheaply and quickly produced to satisfy a market demand, usually for genre paintings and to make a modest income (i.e., to keep soup boiling in the pot). By extension, the term has come to mean any work considered to lack distinctive quality or originality. Almost every continent has a maker of potboilers, although many of them are also well known for more important works.

■ **power**

one of the more crucial conceptions of much postmodern is that things we used to take for granted as given — things like nature and truth — do not have objectively verifiable existence because they are nothing more than paradigms created, unwittingly or not, by broad, impersonal forces in society. For Foucauldians, these forces are determined by epistemes, habits of knowing peculiar to given social groups who have managed to suppress rival groups in practice and who continue to maintain power by instituting symbolic mechanisms which masquerade as disinterested knowledge, but which are really systems intended to keep subjugated those peoples who are uninitiated or excluded.

■ pragmatics, semantics, syntactics

Charles W. Morris developed a three-part structure to clarify the nature of language. 'Pragmatics' he defined as the study of the circumstances in which a communication takes place, ranging from purely material conditions like the presence or absence of noise, to more intangible conditions like personal motivations or the relations between speaker and audience. Pragmatics is thus very close to context. 'Semantics' he defined as the study of meaning in signs prior to their use in a particular statement. While this might suggest that a parallel can be drawn between semantics and iconography, Morris's term is more abstract and closer in meaning to interpretant and paradigm, both of which can be embraced within the term content. 'Syntactics' Morris defined as the study of rules of syntax or grammar, which to some extent is embraced within the term form.

■ prejudice

in common speech, bias or unfair treatment. In Hans-Georg Gadamer's hermeneutic theory — most notably in Truth and Method - - one cannot achieve an objective understanding of the meaning of a work produced under culturally, geographically, historically and/or socially alien circumstances. One can, however, achieve a balanced understanding (and a sort of dialogue between past and present that goes beyond superficial perspectivism) by making oneself fully aware (via a hermeneutic circle) of the conditions and assumptions underlying one's own point of view, as well as those of the author. These conditions he called prejudices or prejudgements.

■ presence

the fact or condition of being present, i.e., of being at hand or before one, of actually existing. In postmodern contexts, presence is caught up in the discussion of determinacy, in the sense that there must be something lurking behind a sign, in order to guarantee that it will signify. In that sense, a determinist would believe in some sort of presence (if only metaphorically). In contrast, deconstruction would argue that there is no such metaphysical guarantee.

■ presentational symbol

Professor Dale Cannon gives this: 'A religious symbol that serves not only to represent some aspect of what is taken to be ultimate reality, but which, in the appropriate circumstances, serves for participants to render it present and enable direct participation in it. In that respect, they are sometimes called sacramental symbols. All presentational symbols are, in the first place, representational symbols, but the reverse is not true'.

■ presentiment

foreboding. Giorgio de Chirico said that an ominous feeling of something about to happen was a characteristic of good metaphysical art. It has been argued that he was directly influenced in this by Freud's uncanny. The idea appears frequently in aesthetic theory, albeit in slightly different forms. Another example is in Jung's notion of the visionary mode of artistic creation.

■ presentment

not a common word, but Edward Bullough used it to denote the manner of presenting something, as distinct from 'presentation', which he understood to mean that which is presented. The word is not to be confused with presentiment either.

■ prestation value

the conventional prestige value of a sign in an otherwise valueless Baudrillardian world of simulacra.

■ primary colours

the basic hues of the spectrum from which all of the other hues can be mixed. The primary colours actually differ from context to context, but in the classic formal language of much artwriting, there are only the three: red, blue and yellow. Classic colour theory asserts that admixtures of any two of these in the proper proportions will result in the creation of 'secondary' colours which will be the 'complementary' of the third primary colour. For example, mixing the primary red and blue gives the secondary violet, which is the complementary of yellow; mixing red and yellow gives orange, the complementary of blue and mixing yellow and blue gives green, the complementary of red. One of the curious optical phenomena attending this observation is that a hue will always seem its most vibrant when accompanied by its complementary.

■ primordial image

the term was coined by Jakob Burckhardt, but it is now most closely associated with C. G. Jung's notion of the archetype.

■ problematic

some writers use this conventionally as an adjective meaning 'ambiguous, capable of creating a problem, doubtful, questionable'.

Writers of Marxist inclination tend to use it more specifically as a noun, meaning the ideological framework within which a particular issue is discussed. For example, the Marxist critique of the art of Gustave Courbet in the early 1850s is driven by the problematic of class struggle.

■ **process**

in some current writing there is a greater emphasis on the mechanisms of creating meaning (the 'process') than on meaning (the 'product') itself, especially when the writer is particularly concerned with ideology.

■ **product semantics**

phrase coined by Reinhart Butter to indicate loosely the semiotics of advertising for the producers of such products. It was used as the title of a conference at the University of Industrial Arts in Helsinki in 1989.

■ **pro homine**

a tactic in informal logic where conclusion X should be accepted because it is held to be true by person Y, who is ostensibly knowledgeable, trustworthy and free of bias. Rarely identified as such, the tactic appears with alarming frequency in some writing about art, alarming because the alleged authority is frequently not above suspicion. An instance which casts connoisseurship in a poor light is a story in which the famed connoisseur Bernard Berenson gave a painting a highly desirable attribution, or, to be more charitable, he did not deny it the attribution because he was pressured to do so by the works' owners.

■ **prolepsis**

an anticipation, as in foreseeing possible objections to an argument in order to answer them in advance. In a different form, this concept is fairly common in current thought, but it is rarely addressed as such.

protagonist

in narrative analysis, the principal character, hero(ine) or leading role. In Angelica Kauffmann's Cornelia, Mother of the Gracchi, the protagonist is Cornelia. In David's Le Sacre, it is Napoleon.

pseudotranshistorical

a commonplace in popular culture for people to assume that certain great works of the past do not really belong to the past but to a perpetual present. Accordingly, for example, Michelangelo's Sistine Chapel ceiling or Leonardo's Mona Lisa appear to be timeless, giving the viewer the opportunity to read into them any meaning they choose. While one component of this enterprise, the undermining of exclusive authorial responsibility for the production of meaning, is generally applauded in postmodernism, it also creates the illusion that the artist intended the work to exist outside of his or her particular historical moment, which is, according to postmodern thought in general, quite impossible. Mieke Bal has added 'pseudo' to show that the impression of timelessness is false.

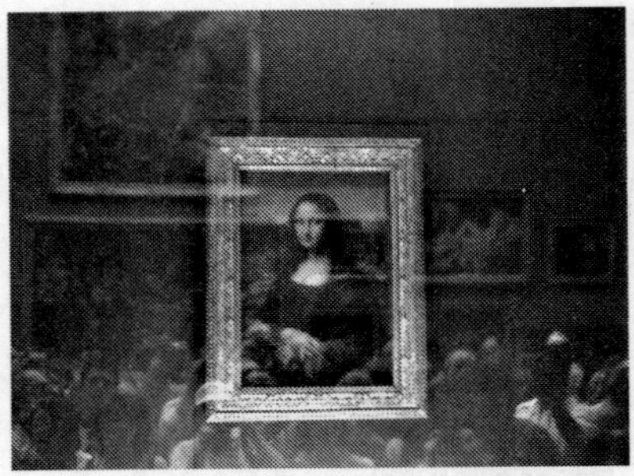

Mona Lisa

psychic embed

Mary Daly's term (in Pure Lust: Elemental Feminist Philosophy) for basic structures of or practices within the female psyche which usually function without the subject's being aware of them. One such is what Demaris S. Wehr called internalised oppression.

psychophysical parallelism

Gottfried Wilhelm Leibniz's response to the mind-body

problem was similar to occasionalism, in that both denied the direct interaction of mind and body. Leibniz, however, did not conclude that the only will was divine intervention, preferring to believe that the mind and the body were ordained to be separate but parallel to one another.

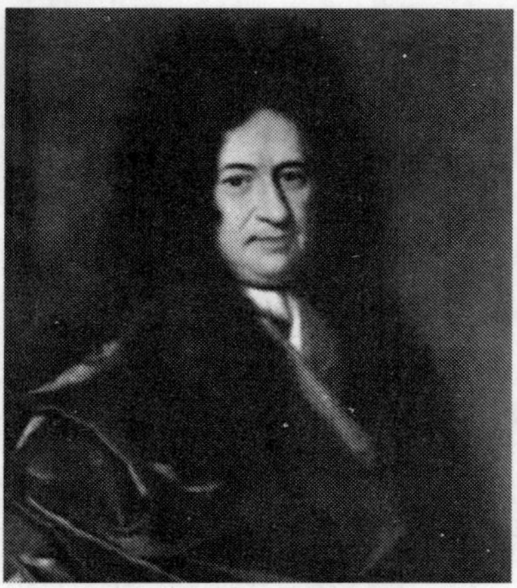

Gottfried wilhelm Leibniz

■ pun

the opposite of double entendre. Where a double entendre is a play on a single word with two or more meanings, a pun is a play on different words with the same sound. When the doctor told the patient who dreamt on alternate nights that he was a wigwam and a teepee that he was 'too tense', the doctor used a pun (one sound, two words). If the doctor had said the patient would feel a prick as soon as he bent over, he would have used a double entendre (one word, two meanings).

■ puritanism

beginning in sixteenth century England as a programme of religious reform, but now associated with any particularly zealous austerity, discipline, frugality, industry and the like. One can discern a Puritan sensibility in most art which favours austerity and it is particularly common in Dutch art, from Baroque-era paintings of plain church interiors to Mondrian's mature works. Most recently, the term has been applied to both sides of the debate on political correctness to explain fairly high degrees of intolerance.

quadrivium
see **liberal arts**.

quality
a degree of excellence or superiority, whether of form or content. Quality in a work of art has become a highly problematic concept from a postmodern point of view, since any notion of what constitutes quality by definition excludes other possibilities, leading some to charge that it is little more than an instrument of imperialism, racism and other forms of oppression. And yet, however vaguely it is defined, some types of criticism, especially connoisseurship and formalism, have relied on it very heavily.

quantohistory
the historical study of patterns of cultural change with the tools and methods of statistical analysis. The approach has made very few inroads into artwriting.

quoin
corner stones in architecture lending strength or other emphasis, distinguished from the rest of the surface by greater size, different colour and/or rustication or the imitation of same in brick or paint.

quotation
the presentation, within one's own work, of a selection or brief passage from another's work and the acknowledgment thereof. This is usually restricted to verbal excerpts from another's work, but it is easily extendable to visual culture, especially in instances of allusion, appropriation and citation.

racism
systematic discrimination and other forms of oppression directed at members of other races. The problem has appeared in art and artwriting in a variety of forms, ranging from descriptions of simple illustrations of the problem, both pro and con, to thorough investigations of whether the canon of mostly DWMs is

part of a larger conspiracy to exclude non-whites.

■ radial balance

a 'pinwheel' balance achieved by contriving parts of an image to spin more or less from a central point. The classic example is Rubens' Rape of the Daughters of Leucippus.

■ read into

colloquial expression referring to the practice of producing meanings in the reverse of what had been thought to be the normal pattern, prior to postmodernism, from artist to work to audience. That is, the viewer tends less to extract what is thought to be 'genuine' meaning from the work in favour of pushing meanings of his or her own back into it. While this phrase has most often been used rather dismissively (as in 'you're just reading into it what you want it to be'), the practice has become commonplace, even valorised, in postmodernism, albeit on a more complex level.

■ real

Lacanian term, originally for what might be expected, the actual and verifiable, as opposed to the imaginary and the symbolic. In later writings, the term has taken on a slightly more developed sense: since everyone operates psychologically within the realm of the symbolic, no one can ever truly gain access to the real, meaning that it is forever just out of reach. In that sense, then, it is not 'verifiable'. Since art can only deal with the imaginary and the symbolic, then, the real in this sense has little utility in artwriting.

■ realism

a highly problematic word with different connotations in different contexts.

1. In popular parlance, it means a generic species of representation that looks real, in the sense that some art history uses the word naturalism. In this sense, re-

alism is the representation of a putatively unmediated world, by whatever means. One of the common themes of postmodernism is a challenge of this still-popular notion.

2. In traditional art history, Realism (with an upper case 'R') denotes the type of realism practiced in the nineteenth century by Gustave Courbet and his successors, often involving some sort of socio-political or moral message, if only by virtue of context.

3. Philosophy provides the third and fourth senses: in scholastic philosophy, realism means what most people understand as 'idealism', i.e., that (more or less Platonic) universals have a genuine, tangible existence.

4. In more modern philosophy, realism is very nearly the exact opposite, the 'common sense' attitude that real objects exist independently of their being observed. Sometimes called 'metaphysical realism', this latter position is cast in doubt by much postmodernism as well.

■ received opinion

a relative consensus about something. Received opinion varies widely, depending upon which group is being investigated. For example, the received opinion about Vincent Van Gogh in the popular imagination is that his art looks the way it does, entirely because of (what is thought to be known of) his state of mind. In such instances, received opinion usually arises without debate or reflection. This is less true of special interest groups. For example, within the art history community, the received opinion about Van Gogh would be more likely to take into account his artistic influences, current art theory, his religious upbringing, etc. Unless qualified in some way, 'received opinion' usually connotes more of the former than the latter and thus says something about the attitudes developed by posterity.

■ receiver
in information theory, the audience or target towards which a communication is intended.

■ red herring
see **irrelevance**.

■ redundancy
in information theory, the desirable repetition of the same message in different codes, so that the receiver can still get the message in spite of noise. In art, one might argue that form and content should harmonise in some way so that, say, expressive brushwork could convey the sense of unease as effectively as a particular choice of subject matter, especially important in an era when audiences seem increasingly unlikely to have had the education or inclination to recognise something specific about the latter. However, it is important not to lose sight of the idea that a lack of redundancy, that is, a supposed failure of form and content to harmonise could have a very desirable effect as well. In many other contexts, the word simply means an undesirable repetition.

■ reference
words are thought to take on meaning in a variety of ways. A common sense approach is that words have some sort of direct relation to the thing they signify, their referent, but only onomatopoeia actually has anything like a direct relation. In Saussurean semiotics, all words are thought to have meaning strictly because of the paradigms in which they find themselves and not because of some imagined reference to the world outside language. Genuine reference, in fact, is denied altogether, which is what makes it possible for deconstruction to exist. Peircean semiotics, in contrast, argues that an icon and an index have meanings determined by their relation

to their referents: i.e., if the sign resembles the referent, it is an icon. If the sign has some existential relationship with the referent, it is an index. For Peirce, only the symbol has as purely arbitrary a relationship as that imagined by Saussure.

■ referent
the thing (event, object, person, etc.) to which an icon, index, symbol or other signifier refers.

■ refusal
occasionally used as a near synonym of subversion.

■ reification
the act of making something abstract into something concrete. In Marxist terminology, reification usually means treating human actions, characteristics and relations as if they were objective things with an independent existence. Religion, for example, is treated as something given to humankind, rather than created by it. In some Marxist writings, reification also means treating humans more or less as things without independent will, responding passively to the dictates of a world of objects.

■ relative
the opposite of absolute. That which has a connection to, dependence upon or relation with something other than itself. In formal terminology, e.g., 'relative scale' means the apparent size of a thing in a given context. An awareness of relative scale is especially important in slide lectures, which show students works of art as if they were all about the same size as the screen.

■ saccade
the movement of the eye from one fixation point to another, for an application peculiar to visual semiotics.

■ sacred
much art has been preoccupied in varying degrees throughout its history with the sacred, conceived as the quintessential identifying characteristic of all divinity, holiness, saintliness, sanctity and the like. But there has recently been a

very sharp turn towards a conception of the sacred deriving from the writings of Emil Durkheim and, more aggressively, Georges Bataille. Describing the sacred as the 'wholly other', i.e., that which is of so fundamentally different an order from common existence that we cannot even describe it, Bataille argued that the sacred therefore springs from the same sources as those things we conventionally find vile, like ritual sacrifice, bodily mutilation, all manner of transgressive activities and even excrement.

■ **salvage paradigm**
a general mode of operation in which a dominant culture, usually Eurocentric, perceives a subordinate culture as dead or dying and attempts to save or salvage it from oblivion. In so doing, the dominant culture usually distorts, mystifies, mythologises or destroys the other culture.

■ **sampling**
technology now permits musicians to make digital recordings of any sound and play them back, thus emulating any combination of instruments or noises, with or without further electronic manipulation. The technique is interesting relative to the history of art for several reasons. Futurist painter Luigi Russolo once wrote a manifesto of music as a new 'art of noise' and he even designed technologically primitive forerunners of today's digital samplers. Sampling also raises the question of copyright or intellectual property and has given rise to several legal cases.

■ **Saussurean**
pertaining to the influential notions of French linguist Fernand de Saussure.

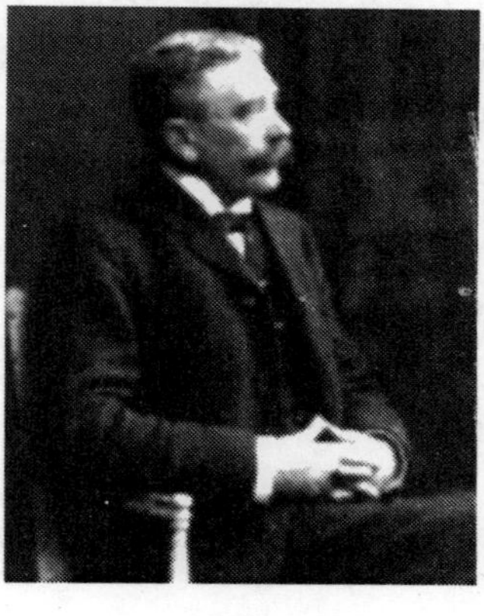

savoir
Lacanian term for knowledge within the symbolic.

saying
see **opening**.

schema
in Art and Illusion, E. H. Gombrich coined the word 'schema' to refer to a diagrammatic depiction of an object or arrangement in space, something along the lines of what we would now call a wireframe drawing, but he also used the word generically to refer to any formulas or standardised devices which could quickly solve pictorial problems. The latter sense is now the most widespread. Although viewers are typically able to identify these devices, when asked, they conventionally suppress their awareness of them in order to experience a coherent illusion.

scientificity
a synonym for disinterestedness .

scopic pulsion
an irresistible urge to look.

scopophilia
the love of looking which underlies and colours much putatively disinterested critical inquiry into visual culture.

scopophobia
the fear of looking, as in castration.

scotoma
a blind spot.

screen wall
see **wall**.

scripto-visual
imagery which has characteristics of both visual art and writing. It could refer to everything from calligraphy (which means 'beautiful writing' and would include Islamic illuminations, Irish bibles and homilies of the sort you see in gift shops) to 'calligraphy-like' imagery (itself ranging from pseudo-writing in visual art, as in Cy Twombly, to actual, legible writing, as in much contemporary feminist autobio-

graphical art, like Mary Kelly, Mary Scott).

secondary colours
see **primary colours**.

section
drawing of the interior of a building, as if vertically sliced midway.

secular humanism
see **humanism**.

self
the self is the subjective sense of being a personal owner of and witness to what neuroscientists call 'mind', to distinguish it from 'brain'. The brain is a physical organ and although its structures and functions are enormously complex, it is an objective entity: that is, multiple observers can independently draw the same conclusions about it, whether simple (for example, its size) or complex (which parts are active at a given moment according to a PET scan or a FMR scan). In contrast, the mind is nothing more than a series of electrochemical events taking place within the brain. Self is another matter. Although we are far from having a clear answer, most recent research suggests that 'self' is little more than an illusion of personal homogeneity which emerges from within the activity of mind. Self, then, will probably remain internal, inscrutable, private. While the components giving rise to it will be determinable, the illusion these components produce is not likely to be susceptible to objective measures in the same way. Like the brain, it can be described as having objective characteristics by multiple observers.

semanalysis
the disruption of 'normal' semiotic procedure by intentionally producing new areas of signification.

seme
when one encounters a word like 'bark' without a context, one cannot be sure whether it refers to a dog noise, a commander shouting orders, the

sheath of a woody stem, the rubbing off of skin or various kinds of boats, etc. As soon as some context is supplied, however, we are able to suspend one or more of the multiple meanings. Like 'bark', most signifiers have clusters of possibilities circulating about them like moths about a flame, but when they come together with other signifiers, elements within one cluster will reinforce similar elements in another. The effect is to foreground a possibility which is more likely than any of the others by virtue of having been activated, as it were, by more than one signifier in the construction. The foregrounded meaning stands out as a kind of path between the other possibilities, which led A. J. Greimas, Roland Barthes and others, to characterise the structure as a 'semic axis'. Semes, then, are basic 'units of meaning constructed from their relational structures alone' due to a 'sorting among contextual variables'.

■ **sememe**

the meaning of a morpheme.

■ **semic axis**

see **seme**.

■ **semiology**

term preferred by the French for semiotics.

■ **semiosis**

the mechanism by which figurative meaning is produced.

■ **semiotics**

deriving from linguistics, semiotics is the study of signs and signifying practices which has, along with deconstruction, feminism, Marxism and a few other critical tendencies, dominated much of the artwriting of the 1980s and 1990s. Modern semiotics began early in the century with the work of two farsighted individuals who were curious as to how structures could produce meaning, as opposed to the resultant meaning itself.

■ **sense**

in his Principles of Semantics (1957), Stephen Ullman uses the word 'sense' in a manner analogous to signified, while 'name' corresponds to signifier. Paul Ricoeur follows the distinction in parts of his Conflict of Interpretations (1974).

■ sensitivity

an imprecise word with various connotations, all relating to a state of high responsiveness or susceptibility to something. The most important implications are 'the capacity of being hurt' (as in the sensitivity of an ethnic group to a racial slur), 'an awareness of the needs and emotions of others' and 'a tolerance towards the marginal' (in questions of political correctness) and 'a particular susceptibility to aesthetic affect' (as in connoisseurship).

■ sexism

discrimination based on gender, although sexism is most often understood as discrimination specifically against women.

■ sfumato

see **chiaroscuro**.

■ shade

see **colour**.

■ show towel

embroidered Mennonite hand-towels intended primarily for display.

■ shuttering

formwork for moulding unset concrete into the desired shape.

■ sign

in Saussurean semiotics, an element of language composed of the relationship between a signifier (a sound-image) and a signified (the idea which is thus expressed). Although the Saussurean model has become the more fashionable, Peircean semiotics is actually better suited to the visual because it accounts more successfully for resemblance. For Peirce, a sign is an element of language composed of the relationship between a the sign itself, a referent (the object to which the sign refers), the 'ground' (the nature of the relationship to the referent, which in turn determines whether the sign is an icon, index or symbol) and the interpretant (the relationship between the interpreter and the meaning).

■ sign proper

phrase sometimes used in place of symbol, as understood in Peircean semiotics.

■ signifiance

not to be confused with significance, Julia Kristeva used this term to mean the mechanisms within language which permit it to deliver more than the simple communication of verifiable facts. Roland Barthes' Image, Music, Text (1977) associated it with the so-called 'third' or 'obtuse meaning', which stands outside the merely 'informational' and 'symbolic' meanings of conventional communication.

■ significance

not to be confused with signifiance, 'significance' has a chain of denotations running from 'importance' to 'purpose' to 'meaning'. In the latter instance, however, a few writers like E. D. Hirsch maintain a strict theoretical distinction between (unintended) 'significance' and (intended) meaning.

■ significant form

Clive Bell's vaguely defined term indicating what he saw as the essential characteristic of all art, relations and combinations of aesthetically moving formal elements, regardless of the circumstances of its production or the era in which it was made.

■ signified

in Saussurean semiotics, the idea (or 'meaning', in the simplest sense of the word) expressed by a particular signifier. The two together constitute a sign.

■ signifier

in Saussurean semiotics, the sound-image (or other form of vehicle) which conveys a signified. According to Saussure, although the two together constitute a sign, they have only an arbitrary relationship. That is, while the letters 'r', 'e' and 'd', when presented in a particular order, are taken to denote a certain colour, neither the letters themselves nor their formal combination have anything to do with redness.

■ signifying economy

a signifying economy is the system of exchange within an identifiable group that pertains to meanings. It thus has much to do with how meaning is a function of a horizon of expectations. For example, the signifying economy of the seventeenth-century, Netherlands, as different from that of today, so their still-life paintings of flowers had different sorts of meanings for them than they do for us. One of the goals of traditional art history has always been to reconstruct the original values of the signifying economy, so that we can understand what works meant when they were made.

■ signifying practice

a common phrase in current artwriting and cultural analysis. For example, in La Traversée des signes and elsewhere, Julia Kristeva uses this phrase to mean the simultaneous creation and interrogation of any system of signs. The creation of the system evokes a subject within a particular social formation and the disruption of the system challenges that social formation. Her emphasis on process clearly gives greater weight to the signifier than to the signified.

■ situation

name of an exhibition in London, England, in 1960 of paintings created according to very restrictive rules, like complete abstraction and large scale.

■ situationism

not to be confused with situation, situationism was a proto-punk manifestation of extreme irreverence, contempt for boredom and bourgeois domesticity and artistic freedom of expression, very much influenced by Dada and Surrealism's spirit of poetically expressive revolt. Although the so-called Situationist International began in 1957, it only became a subject of widespread discussion in the 1990s, with the English translation of guiding light Guy Debord's Comments on the Society of the Spectacle.

■ **scepticism**

often mistaken for cynicism and mere naysaying, scepticism is more productively the attitude, philosophy and practice of critical thinking, i.e., informal logic, in everyday life.

■ **slice-of-life**

a type of synecdoche, that is, an arbitrary cropping of a scene, especially common in Impressionism and in snapshot photography, where figures or important motifs might be interrupted by the edge of the image or by something interposed between them and the camera. The device suggests a momentary glimpse of reality, rather than a carefully composed, formal imitation of it.

■ **snapshot**

an informal photograph displaying ostensibly amateur characteristics, like accidental compositions, momentary glimpses of quotidian events and sometimes even technical problems.

■ **social formation**

the social context (embracing the economic, moral, political and other expectations of a given group) in which a language produces a shared meaning specific to the time and place. The term is close in meaning to horizon of expectations.

■ **social practice**

the notion that art of whatever sort is produced in and for a given social formation, rather than as an indulgence in pure self- expression or self-exorcism.

■ **sociolinguistics**

the study of linguistics as lived experience, i.e., of language as it is actually used in identifiable social contexts.

■ sociological criticism
umbrella term for a variety of interpretive approaches foregrounding environmental or secondary context, i.e., the circumstances of production outside the artist's control, but not necessarily applied to material considered historical.

■ soffitt
1. the underside of a projected eave.
2. a synonym for intrados.

■ sophisticated
an antonym for vulgar. Where a vulgar Marxist is concerned principally with a superficial description of, say, market forces and their impact on class consciousness, a sophisticated Marxist interweaves these ideas with a more complex consideration of such things as ideology, psychology and even deconstruction . It has been said that it is only their understanding of 'vulgar' as disdainful that prevents respectful sophisticated Marxists from applying the term to Marx himself.

■ source analysis
classical source analysis, one of the more long-standing and widespread approaches in traditional art history, is the study of artists' allusions to and appropriations of the work of earlier artists. The analyst hopes to discover if the later artist's sources indicate admiration, citation, emulation or simply a learning experience.

■ space-time
an imprecise term indicating the prevalent conditions of time and place in a work.

■ spatter
a decorative motif achieved by random distribution of accidental driblets, usually described with more pretentious terms when applied to high art.

■ specificity
distinctiveness in time and place, the particular nature of any phenomenon or the

uniqueness of a response to a particular set of circumstances. Most postmodern thought emphasises historical specificity, which challenges those outdated concepts like genius, masterpiece and timelessness which share the opposed idea that some things can be universal or transhistorical.

■ **spectacular**

conventionally, something which is especially dramatic or impressive. In some writing, in contrast, it means simply any public display (as in punk clothing), which has features distinguishing it from other public displays (as in business suits), although all might be quite unspectacular in the conventional sense.

■ **specular**

having the properties of a mirror.

■ **spin**

colloquial term indicating paralinguistic inflection or connotations accruing to an image, word, etc.

■ **spin doctor**

colloquial term indicating a public relations person hired to shape public perception, particularly of political persons, parties and situations. There has never been a shortage of art critics willing to serve in this capacity for artists. A careful reader will distinguish between such a critic and a less subservient voice.

■ **split**

see **split subject**.

■ **split subject**

since Freud, consciousness has been divided into more than one level. 'Split subject' is simply the heterogeneous nature of the real psyche, as described by such writers as Julia Kristeva, as opposed to the illusion of wholeness signified by unary subject.

■ **spontaneity**

once a watchword of advanced art interested in unpremeditated self-expression, spontaneity is now regarded with suspicion. Theodor Adorno was one of the earliest to say why, although his example is actually jazz music: since mass culture in the era of capitalism works by offering ever-increasing sensual happiness in the here and now, spontaneity in the arts is really just an expression of the desire created in the populace by ideology.

■ **statement**
sometimes used as a translation for énoncé.

■ **stipulative definition**
non-standard, personal or other specific connotations of a term in a given context, usually overtly laid out as diverging from dictionary standards.

■ **story**
in current semiotics, 'story' is a near synonym of diegesis, the apparent narrative as it is produced in the mind of the reader, rather than literally on the page.

■ **stratigraphic fallacy**
in The Interpretation of Cultures, Clifford Geertz argued against the establishment of an anthropological hierarchy of human behaviour, with biology as its base and successive psychological, social and finally, cultural strata. The image such a scheme gave of culture was that of an afterthought, not an integral part of the human condition. To oppose this stratigraphic fallacy, he proposed the notion of 'webs of significance' which spun their way throughout various levels without prioritising them. Anthropology was thus in his mind not an experimental science in search of law but an interpretive science in search of meaning.

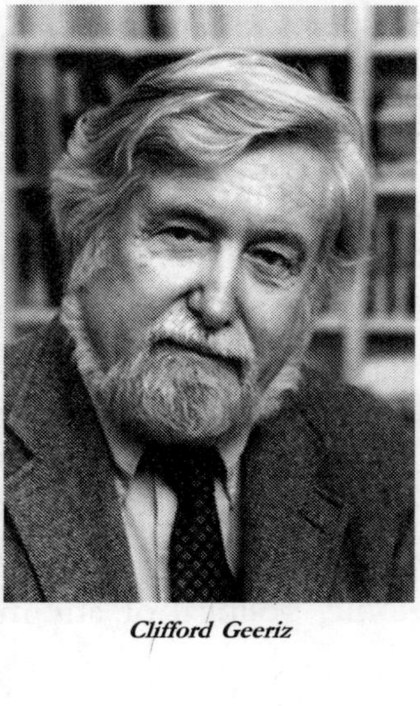

Clifford Geeriz

■ structuralist marxism
term sometimes applied to Althusser's method of describing human individuals not as having some essential characteristics but as the product of social determinants, taking the form of some sort of social structure, as in class consciousness, for example.

■ stylisation
any manner of representation putting greater emphasis on the method of expression than on the appearance of nature. This includes the Egyptian canon of proportions, the conventional drapery patterns in Byzantine icons, Cubist fragmentation of figures into interpenetrating planes and so on.

■ subculture
conventionally, any group sharing characteristics which are distinctive enough to differentiate them from other groups within a larger or 'parent' culture. These characteristics may be economic, ethnic, political or any matter of lifestyle. More particularly, 'subculture' is used to designate those smaller groups which function in opposition to the larger culture, as in the punk subculture discussed in Dick Hebdige's Subculture: The Meaning of Style (1979). Stuart Hall (et al., Resistance Through Rituals [1976]) distinguishes subculture, which he sees as informally and intuitively organised, from 'counter-culture', which he sees as more formally arranged and more expressly political and consciously ideological. In this scheme, punks were sub cultural and hippies were counter-cultural.

■ subject
1. older writings will use this word to indicate an issue, theme or topic, as in subject matter or to indicate a body of knowledge, as in the subjects one studies at school.
2. recent ones, particularly those influenced by psychoanalytical criticism, are more

likely to use it exclusively as 'agent', an entity that acts, thinks and feels.

■ subject in process

a near synonym of split subject.

■ subjective

characteristic of reality as perceived, rather than as objectively true outside of the mind. This would include such things as objects and events experienced in a manner peculiar to a particular individual (and therefore not reproducible, in the manner of an objective scientific inquiry). This is what most speakers mean when they say that interpretation, for example, is purely subjective.

■ subject matter

the old definition of this as 'the topics or themes in a work as distinct from the style in which they are presented' is no longer tenable since the form of an artwork is one of the factors constitutive of its content. A simple distinction between subject matter and content is not detailed enough to transcribe the mechanisms of signification.

■ subject presumed to know

a phrase that appears in Jacques Lacan's écrits, sometimes translated 'subject who is presumed (or supposed) to know'. Generally, it indicates that a subject can only presume to have achieved objective knowledge. Specifically, it warns psychoanalysts not to be seduced by the illusion that they fully understand everything about a patient, an effect brought about by the patient's growing self-awareness but attributed to the analyst through transference. The idea should be kept in mind when psychoanalytic criticism is applied to art.

■ sublimation

in Freudian and Lacanian thought, the process of diverting the energy of a drive, such as a sexual urge, to some other, ostensibly more elevated or socially acceptable realm, such as aesthetic activity. For example, Nietzsche felt that Raphael's Madonnas could only be the result of the sublimation of his passions.

■ sublime

Edmund Burke's Philosophical Enquiry into the Origin of Our Ideas of the Sublime and the Beautiful (1757) identified the Sublime (usually capitalised today) as something so vast, grand or dangerous that it could only inspire awe, fear or veneration.

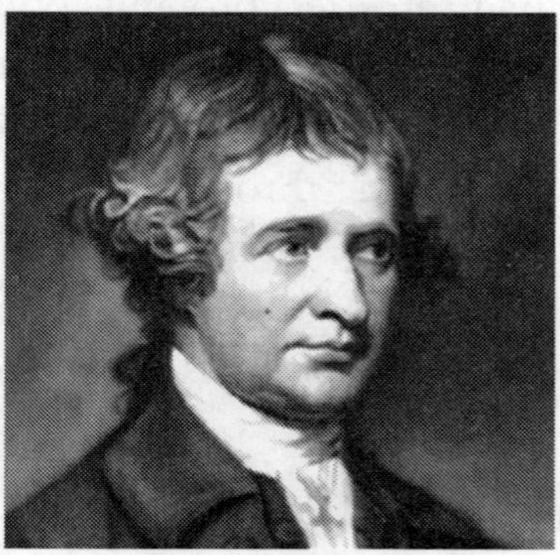

Edmund Burke

■ subliminal

below normal thresholds, as in a sound vibrating at a frequency below the normal range of human hearing. In the 1970s, there was a great deal of discussion of subliminal messages in advertising, particularly in the books of Brian Wilson Keye (Subliminal Seduction). Ostensibly, all sorts of hidden communications, usually about sex, offered enticements to buy a given product, but they were themselves below the level of conscious reception. Some critics may also be taking something of this sort for granted in their artwriting, for they occasionally discover meanings which seem to have little to do with objectively describable features of a given work.

■ subversion

any act intended to overthrow or undermine something, usually in situations where the thing overthrown is seen as oppressive, as in intervention.

■ sufficiency

in informal logic, the notion that premises must be complete enough to account for a given conclusion. For example, an extensional definition that identifies a sculpture only as 'something one can walk around' is insufficient because one can walk around a house, a shopping mall or the block. Similarly, in the syllogism 'The photographer hates models who are late; I am not late; therefore, the photographer will not hate me' is insufficient because the photographer might hate the model for some other, unstated reason.

■ super

a colloquial expression for superimposed titles and/or credits in television production. Some contemporary painting makes use of a similar idea, with words placed directly over other imagery in the manner seen in television and print advertisements. Examples include David Salle, Annette Lemieux, Barbara Kruger and innumerable others.

■ supplement

in Derridean thought, the 'extra' clusters of meaning normally screened out by the action of semic axes but retrieved by deconstruction.

■ surface structure

see **deep structure and surface structure**.

■ surfiction

another word for metafiction and title of a Raymond Federman study of same.

■ syllogism

an elementary structure in informal logic, along the classic Aristotelian lines of 'All humans are mortal; all artists are human; therefore, all artists are mortal'.

■ symbol

1. conventionally, something used for or conceived of as representing something else, as an 'x' symbolises a variable in an equation or a dog symbolises fidelity, etc.

2. in Peircean semiotics, a symbol is one of three basic types of signs, the other two being the icon and the index. The ground of the relationship between an icon and its referent is resemblance and

the ground of the relationship between an index and its referent is causal or existential. For those signs with a relationship to a referent that is purely arbitrary and conventional, Peirce reserved the term 'symbol', as a flag symbolises 'patriotism' or a red octagon symbolises 'stop'.

■ **symbolic**

Lacanian term to designate the most basic psychological processes, in which the sense of self is forever under construction in the midst of a network of signifying structures initiated during the mirror stage and inevitably involving the realm of the social. In other words, there is no self without another.

■ **synchronic**

see **diachronic**, **linguistics**.

■ **synecdoche**

one of the four major tropes, synecdoche is the poetic use of a part to signify the whole and, somewhat less frequently, the use of a whole to signify a part. Even in common speech, we encounter phrases like 'all hands on deck' or 'there were forty head grazing in the pasture'. In art, far from being a mere visual accident, the device is chiefly used for dramatic effect or for controlling the viewer's degree of awareness of details, as in the barrels of guns anonymously poking in from the right side of one of Goya's Disasters of War prints.

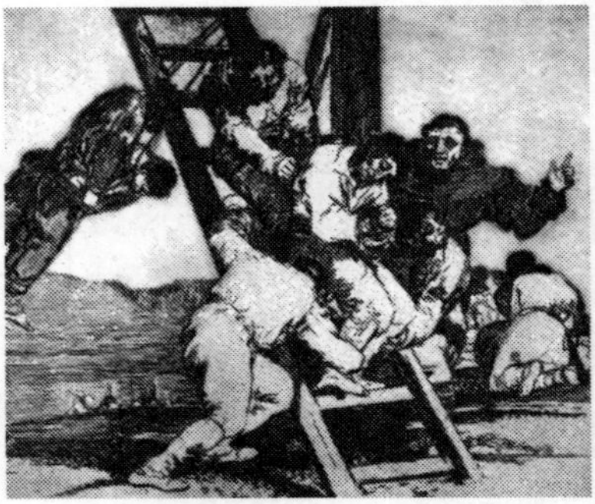

Goya's Disaster of War

■ **syntactics**

see **pragmatics, semantics, syntactics.**

■ **syntagm**

the polar opposite of paradigm where 'paradigm' indicates the relationship of a word to other words outside of a given utterance, 'syntagm' indicates the relationship of a word to other words within a given utterance. The 'syntagmatic axis' is thus basically grammar. In film studies, the syntagmatic axis is the succession of images, so that a metaphor, for example, in a syntagmatic axis means one which emerges across a sequence of views.

■ syntagmatic axis
see **syntagm**.

■ tachisme
see **action painting**.

■ teach the conflict
at the heart of the political correctness, debate centres is the question of how to deal with a Eurocentric canon without simply caving in to the demands of pressure groups (which would merely set a precedent entailing caving in again in a few years, when new groups succeed them). Gerald Graff's solution is simply to teach the conflict itself. If nothing else, it will show that it is possible to live with difference and to do so without xenophobia or closed-mindedness.

■ tectonic
pertaining to building, having an obvious structure, a work in another medium (e.g., a painting) characterised by horizontal and vertical emphases, as in a building. Mondrian's mature works are obviously tectonic.

■ teleology
the doctrine that things develop purposively towards an end determined by the thing under development, as a being might move towards individual self-fulfilment or a species towards its ostensible perfection. This would be in contrast to a mechanistic evolution without purpose. The idea lurks behind the theory of formalism, as if art will emerge at some end point of complete and perfect 'artness'. This kind of thinking is behind the complaint of the 1960s that

Miminalism represented the death of art.

■ tenor

1. the general line of thought, as in the tenor of an argument or the drift of a conversation. Any generalisation of the character of an artwork, e.g., its theme or general flavour, might be so described.

2. in the literary writings of I. A. Richards, a tenor is the idea being expressed in a metaphor, as opposed to the vehicle which expresses it.

■ tension

in architecture, the forces tending to stretch certain members, as in the thrust on the centre portion of a wide lintel. In other arts, a precarious balance established between opposing formal features or other elements, usually for some aesthetic effect.

■ testability

in 'The Testability of an Interpretation' (in J. Margolis's Philosophy Looks at the Arts), Monroe C. Beardsley argues that some interpretations are by nature better than others. The best interpretation is therefore the 'right' one. The criteria for testing interpretations are analogous to those under the heading validity.

■ text

originally referring simply to a body of writing, its use in postmodernist contexts is closer to its origins in the Latin texere, to weave. Roland Barthes distinguished between a 'work', which he characterised as a finite body with a determinate meaning and a 'text', which was indeterminate, open-ended and endlessly subject to reinterpretation as audiences changed. As such, 'text' can refer to any expression, consciously artistic or otherwise, which can be read, i.e., which is 'lisible', whether it is written or visual.

■ textbook

the textbook is a troublesome thing in the postmodern era because it is a single object which purports to be a body of essential knowledge as well as implicitly the principal methodology for dealing with its subject. That is, it is both 'what to know' and 'how to know it'. As a result, it can serve as a good example of one institution's type of power.

■ textuality

see **intertextuality**.

■ texture

1. the surface characteristics of an object. These can be tactile, in the sense of a physical texture in actuality or visual, in the sense of an illusionistic rendering of a texture in a virtually flat painting or photograph.
2. more loosely, the identifying character of a work, its flavour, mode, mood, tone or voice. Both senses can have strong affective properties.

■ Third World other

Gayatri Spivak's term to describe any non-European people with an intact material culture which can be recovered and exploited, either interpretively or in terms of commodity fetishism by Eurocentric interests.

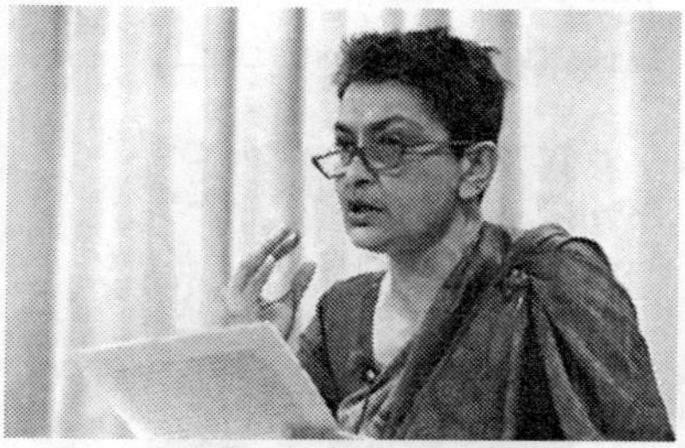

Gayatri Spivak

■ thought police

popular media term of disdain for those in favour of some variation of political correctness.

■ thrust

the downward pressure of architectural weight.

■ timelessness

the notion that certain works of art are so filled with genius that they rise above the specifics of time and place to occupy a transcendental, superhuman plane of existence that does not belong to history. This idea, sometimes also called 'transhistorical' (e.g., in Herbert Marcuse's

The Aesthetic Dimension) and apparently still fashionable among the general populace, is rejected by postmodernism in general as pseudotranshistorical.

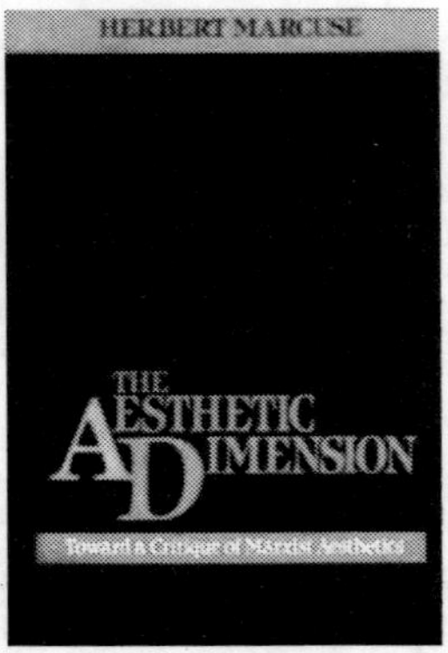

■ **tint**

see **colour**.

■ **topoi**

see **topos**.

■ **topos**

from the Greek koinos topos, 'common place', meaning a standard rhetorical theme or topic. In current artwriting, the term typically concerns a work's content. Older writings sometimes include parallels to culturally determined patterns of configuration (i.e., impulses to use set forms in the expression of stock themes), as in W. Eugene Kleinbauer's characterisation of Aby Warburg's Pathosformel in Modern Perspectives in Art History.

■ **torsion**

twisting or bending, especially in buildings of great height.

■ **toxic**

poisonous. By extension, the principal characteristic of anything deleterious to the health or well being. Although its most frequent use is in 'toxic waste', the word is now tossed about as a basic synonym for dysfunctional in numerous contexts, like 'toxic relationships', 'toxic shame' and so on. Toxic art would presumably be art with a negative affect.

■ **trace**

discussing différance, Jacques Derrida states that each element (for example, a signifier) 'is related to something other than itself [i.e., a signified] but retains the mark of a past element...'.

The various kinds of marks which thus cast doubt on our certainty about the relation between an element and its meaning he calls traces.

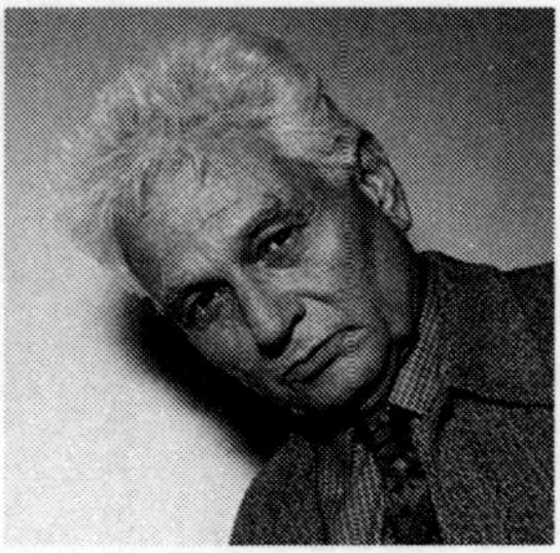

Jacques Derrida

■ tracing

the copying of any form of illustration, drawing, diagram, etc., by covering it with a sheet of transparent or translucent paper or other material and registering its principle (and usually linear) elements thereon.

■ tranche-de-vie

French for slice-of-life.

■ transcendental

characteristic of things which go beyond material existence. The term has two distinct senses in postmodernism, both of which are taken to be fundamental errors. The first is a near synonym for timelessness and it is treated with scepticism. The second describes the traditional logocentric attitude in which the meaning of an utterance is guaranteed in some magical way by a kind of transcendental presence hovering behind the words themselves.

■ transcription

the representation of speech sounds by means of phonetic symbols. There have been several attempts to devise related practices for visual images. A recent example is included in Fernande Saint-Martin's Semiotics of Visual Language.

■ transhistorical

see **timelessness**.

■ transliteration

the representation of a word in the characters of another alphabet, as in transliterations from Cyrillic to English.

triptych
see **altarpiece**.

trompe l'oeil
illusionism, most commonly in painting, but also in some sculpture, etc., intended to 'fool the eye'.

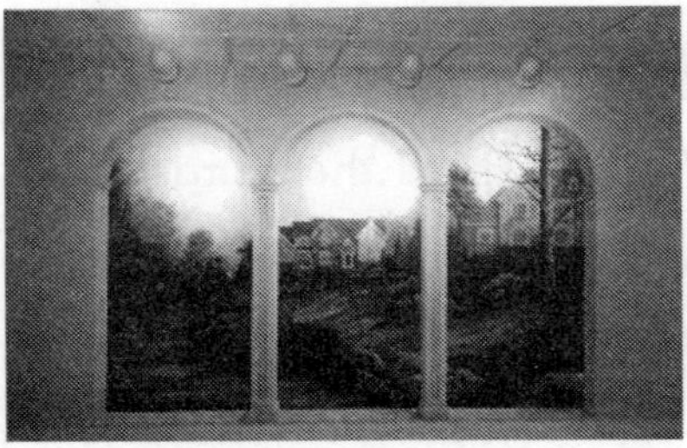

trope
any of several types of diversion from the literal to the figurative. The so-called 'four master tropes' are irony, metaphor, metonymy and synecdoche, but one would have to add parody to this list.

trivium
see **liberal arts**.

truss
extremely strong, usually triangular arrangements of struts.

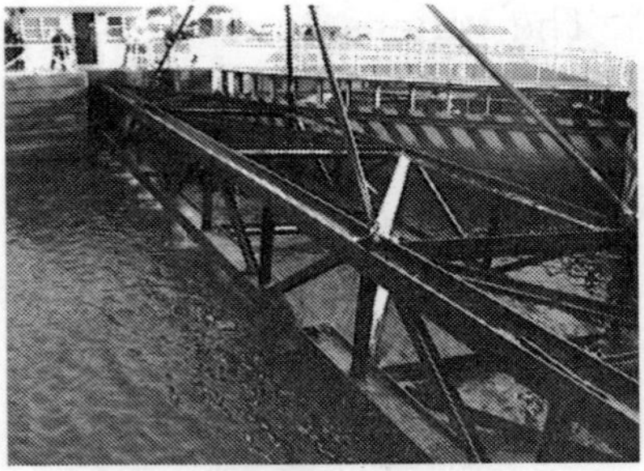

typological study
any of various types of study which approach a given category of content as a thematic block. The practice has its roots in studies of medieval art for the simple reason that analogies between Old and New Testament characters and stories had for centuries been treated as typological parallels. For example, the story of Jonah being swallowed by a whale for three days was interesting to medieval and Renaissance artists principally because it was a prophecy of Christ's entombment and resurrection.

unary subject
Julia Kristeva's term for the erroneous notion that consciousness is some sort of

unified whole. At best, she regards it as a momentary blockage of the disruptive drives characteristic of the real psyche, evident in the split subject.

■ **unbidden**

uncommissioned works produced on spec, as it were.

■ **underpainting**

Artlex gives this: Underpainting: The layer or layers of colour on a painting surface applied before the overpainting or final coat. There are many types of underpainting. One type is an all-over tinting of a white ground. Another is a blocked out image in diluted oil colours that serves as a guide for the painter while developing the composition and colour effects.

■ **unheimlichkeit**

see **Uncanny**.

■ **unique aesthetic emotion**

Clive Bell's vague conception of the rarefied sentiment experienced when examining a true work of art. The conception does not hold up well under close inspection.

■ **universal human interest**

many canons appear to have been constructed with the idea that certain things, works of literature or art, are of such great quality that they belong to no particular time and place or no specific ethnic group or culture. They are thus granted the status of timelessness, in which case they are supposed to be of universal human interest. The critique of institutions, multiculturalism, political correctness and postmodernism in general all deny that such a state exists, apart from those political situations in which groups in power seek to control knowledge in order to suppress other groups. In such an instance, what appears to be timeless is actualy pseudotranshistorical.

unlimited semiosis

a hypothetically infinite process by which one sign or set of signs can take the place of another sign or set of signs which in turn can be replaced by yet another sign or set of signs and so on. Without such polysemy, artists and poets would soon run out of figurative images like tropes. The inexhaustible production of new meanings that results, is a key concept in the semiotics of Umberto Eco and in deconstruction.

unpack

occasionally used as a synonym for 'analyse' or 'deconstruct' in the context of deconstruction . That is, to unpack something is to reveal its layers of hidden meaning.

utilitarianism

a doctrine that the useful is the good and that the determining consideration of right conduct should be the usefulness of its consequences, specifically a theory that the aim of action should be the largest possible balance of pleasure over pain or the greatest happiness of the greatest number.

utopia

a perfect, remote and almost unthinkably ideal 'place' (construed as a location, an era, a political state or even a state of mind) and therefore the opposite of dystopia. Pictorial instances of utopian scenes are fairly commonplace, ranging from Arcadian vistas of the golden age (Greco-Roman wall paintings, some of the landscapes of Poussin and Pierre Puvis de Chavannes, etc.) to almost bizarre visions of an afterlife (Girodet's Ossian Receiving the Napoleonic Officers [1802] comes to mind).

validity

1. in informal logic, validity is determined by whether or not the conclusion of an argument follows necessarily from its premises. If the premises of a valid analytic argument are true, the conclusion must be true. If the pre-

mises of a synthetic argument are true, relevant and sufficient, the conclusion is likely to be true.

2. in a widely read book entitled Validity in Interpretation, E. D. Hirsch argued against what has become the standard postmodern disclosure of multiple meanings (polysemy) by asserting that certain interpretations were more valid than others, particularly those which allowed the author, rather than the work and/or its affect on the audience, to have authority in the determination of meaning.

■ vanitas

the general term applied to a category of subject matter expressing the folly of vanity and the belief in the permanence of healthy existence, beauty and the like. Vanitas themes include such things as beautiful young women confronting death in the form of a skeletal figure (e.g., Anton Wiertz), figures meditating over skulls or skeletons (Georges De La Tour), withering flowers (a host of seventeenth century Dutch still-life artists), children blowing bubbles (Chardin, Paul Peel) and so on. The category is one of the more common in all of pre-modern Western art history.

■ vault

any of various types of arched ceiling. A 'barrel' vault is like an arch increased in depth to create a simple tunnel. While quite effective for some purposes, the disadvantage of a barrel vault is that any penetration of it, as for windows, weakens its ability to withstand thrust. This disadvantage is alleviated when two or more barrel vaults are run into each other to create a 'groin' vault: there, the weakness of the one barrel is compensated for by the other.

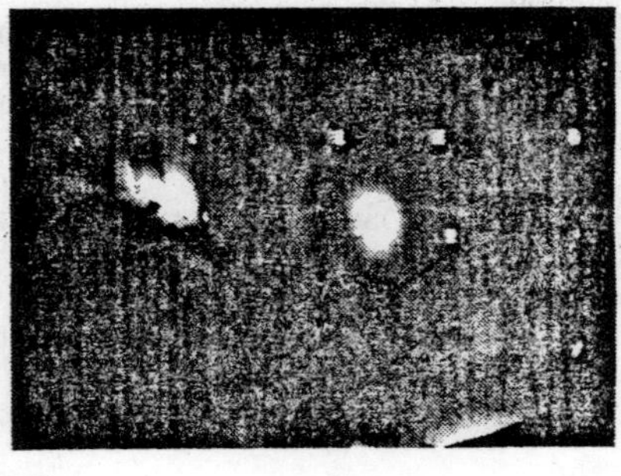

■ vehicle

in the literary theory of I. A. Richards, the means by which a metaphor exploits something familiar in order to convey poetically an adequate impression of something unfamiliar.

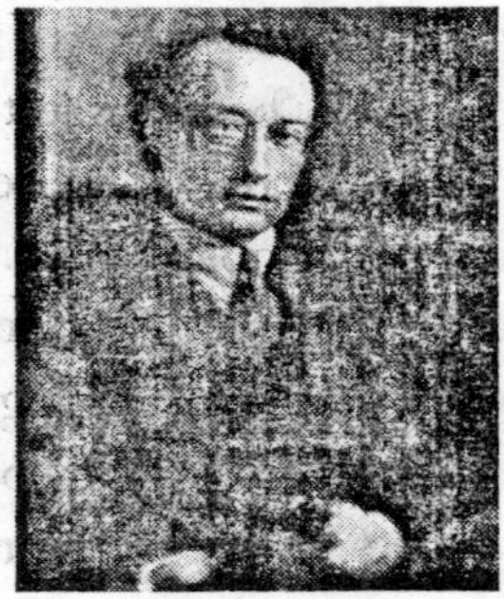

I. A. Richards

■ vehicle shift

by analogy with paradigm shift, a vehicle shift is the point at which certain types of vehicle become too much of a cliché to operate effectively in the production of expressive metaphor. For example, the standard vanitas vehicles had become so conventional by the early nineteenth century that those indifferent to academic thought sought new vehicles for old tenors in natural appearances.

■ verification

Karl Popper argued that nothing could ever be proven true once and for all, since no one could ever be sure that there was no exception to the rule. A statement like 'all swans are white' would only appear to be true to those who had never seen a black one. Popper concluded that the scientific method could not proceed by verification but only by falsification. That is, one would know the statement 'all swans are white' was false as soon as one saw a black swan.

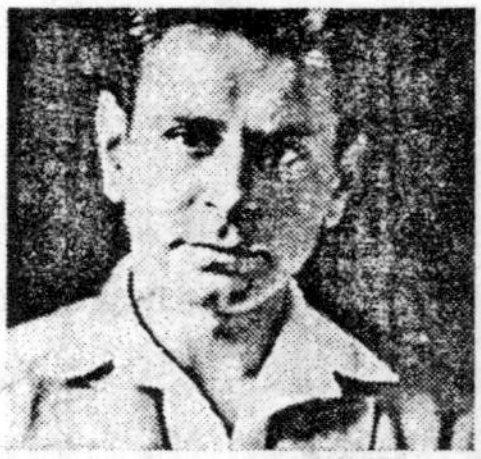

Karl Popper

■ verisimilitude

the degree to which something seems to be true, used of the putative accuracy of a representation.

■ vernacular

a common popular or regional variation from international, academic or other 'accepted' standard usage in language, architecture, etc.

■ victimarchy

word coined by Warren Farrell in The Myth of Male Power to describe a society which conceives of its members as victims, perpetually unable to direct their own affairs or to control their own destinies. In other words, both men and women are victims of patriarchy.

■ visigoths in tweed

derogatory synonym for the cultural left coined for use in the popular media by Dinesh D'Souza.

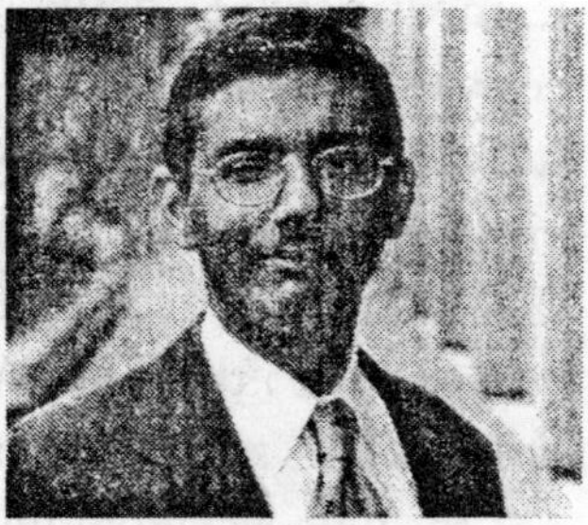

■ visual culture

the body of cultural artefacts which are experienced principally through vision, without the traditional academic separation between high and low culture. Books which deal with visual culture are as comfortable discussing film stills, advertisements, political posters, graffitti and the like as they are in discussing the works of fine art. More importantly, perhaps, the terminology and conceptual assumptions about the ways in which meanings are produced are the same.

■ visual language

see **language**, **semiotics**.

■ vital import

Suzanne Langer's conception of art as presentational symbols, precludes fixed, determinate content, so she replaces the notion of conclusive meaning with vital import, which is the non-objective communication of emotional significance. This is similar to Barthes' notion of the third or obtuse meaning.

■ vulgar

1. see **vernacular**.

2. coarse, lacking in cultivated manners or taste, as in vulgar arts.

3. facile and superficial, when applied as an adjective to certain critical methodologies, especially Marxism. There, it derives from Marx's use of the phrase 'vulgar economics' in Das Kapital, by which he meant a simple study of rather cosmetic phenomena, often veiling an implicit defence of the bourgeois status quo.

wainscotting

decorative panelling on interior walls, usually confined to the lower half.

wall

in architecture, any of a variety of upright structures whose length is many times greater than its thickness and the purpose of which is either support or enclosure. The former, typical in most eras except the High Gothic and the Modern, carries the weight of whatever rests upon it, like the upper stories of a building or a vault. Such a structure is said to be a 'bearing' wall because it bears a load. Examples of the latter include free-standing barriers (like the Great Wall of China) and enclosures which bear loads by other mechanisms.

wampum

beads, usually of shell, strung together and used as a decorative means of exchange in some aboriginal North American cultures.

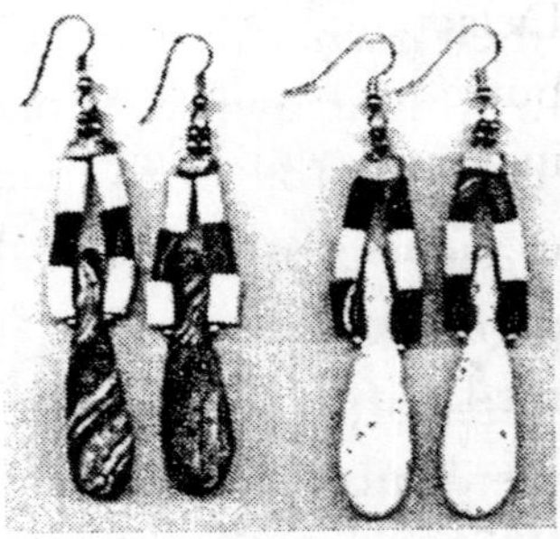

warm colour

reds and yellows and their intermediaries (i.e., oranges) are conventionally referred to as warm colours, ostensibly by virtue of their resemblance to the natural hue of fire and other hot things. Warm colours are said to advance, i.e., to draw towards the foreground of an image and so are said to be generally opposed to the temperature and movement of cool colour.

wash

a layer of thinned colour applied by brush, often rapidly, to roughly block in and/or model forms in paintings, watercolours and some drawings. Famous applications range from colourful watercolour notes, as in the Moroccan sketchbooks of Delacroix, to the colourless but equally adept modelling in Tiepolo drawings.

watercolour

pigment in a water-soluble medium, handled as a wash. Most watercolours are quite translucent and exploit effects peculiar to the medium, like reserve highlights and the appearance of spontaneous and rapid execution.

weltanschauung

the mind-set , outlook or 'world-view' of a particular group, whether aesthetic, ethnic, political, social, etc. Weltanschauungen are usually limited in scope to readily identifiable historical, geographical, ethnic and other entities.

western

1. pertaining to the culture, history and values of the Occidental world, especially Europe and North America. The western mind-set, for example, has been characterised as patriarchal, racist and rationalistic.

2. in literature, film and theatre, works dealing with the western United States of the nineteenth-century, along with its trademark themes of 'cowboys and Indians', pioneering and expansionism, etc. One of the more notable Western artists is Frederick Remington.

woman as the not-yet

Luce Irigaray challenges gender essentialism by arguing that woman is not biologically determined but is caught up in ceaselessly changing cultural productions of gendered meanings. It is possible to negate these productions as they arise, but it is not possible to fix the feminine, so woman is 'woman as the not-yet'.

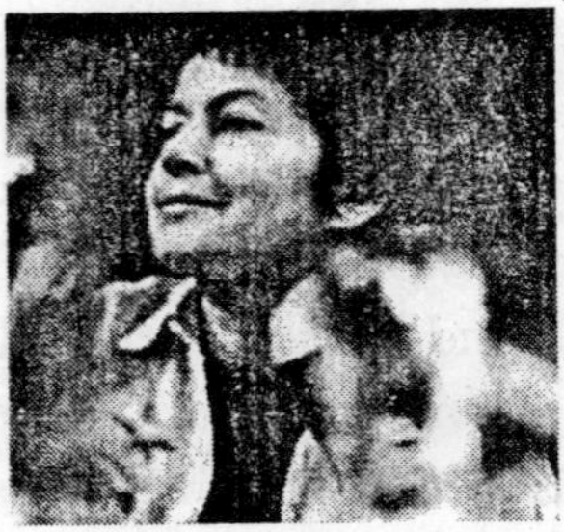

Luce Irigaray

■ **xenophilia**

love of the foreign or unfamiliar. In the 1990s, there was a marked preoccupation in criticism and curatorial practices to valourise everything but the practices of DWMs, i.e., works by women, non-whites and the dispossessed.

■ **xenophobia**

irrational fear or hatred of anything foreign or unfamiliar, especially other social or ethnic groups.

■ **zeitgeist**

in Geistesgeschichte, the Zeitgeist is the spirit of the times, Zeit meaning time and Geist (akin to 'ghost') meaning spirit, intellect and other ephemeral aspects of the psyche. As such, the term is usually taken to mean the general trend of thought or sentiment which supposedly circulates through all the cultural productions of an identifiable era. For example, the Zeitgeist of the Neoclassical period has been characterised as rationalism, whereas that of the Romantic period is sentiment. The Zeitgeist of the early modern period may have been faith in salvation through technological advancement, whereas that of the postmodern period would be disdain for such expressions of certainty in general. Because the identification of a Zeitgeist tends to obliterate difference and imply a degree of essentialism, it is safe to say that postmodern thought in general distrusts it.

■ **ziggurat**

a pyramid with stepped, rather than sloped, sides. The most famous examples were built in early Mesopotamian times.

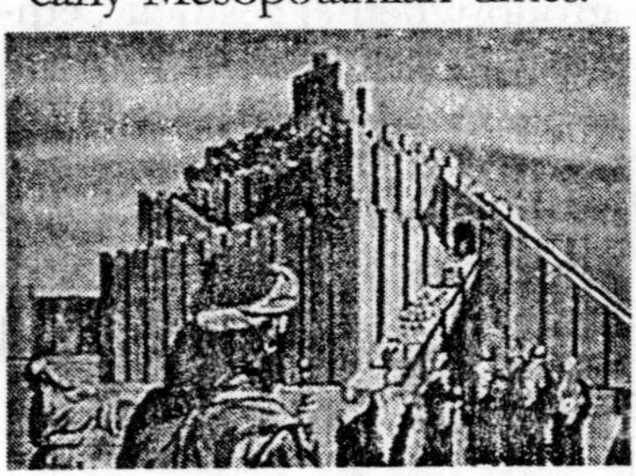